D0386490

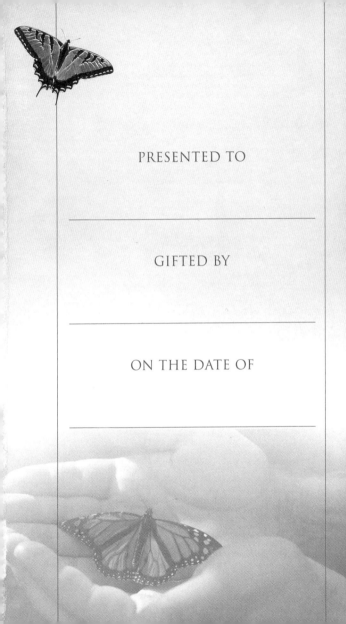

PRESENTED TO

_____

GIFTED BY

_____

ON THE DATE OF

_____

The quoted ideas expressed in this book (but not Scripture verses) are not, in all cases, exact quotations, as some have been edited for clarity and brevity. In all cases, the author has attempted to maintain the speaker's original intent. In some cases, quoted material for this book was obtained from secondary sources, primarily print media. While every effort was made to ensure the accuracy of these sources, the accuracy cannot be guaranteed. For additions, deletions, corrections, or clarifications in future editions of this text, please write Freeman-Smith.

Scripture quotations are taken from:

The Holy Bible, King James Version (KJV)

The Holy Bible, New International Version (NIV) Copyright © 1973, 1978, 1984, by International Bible Society. Used by permission of Zondervan Publishing House. All rights reserved.

The Holy Bible, New King James Version (NKJV) Copyright © 1982 by Thomas Nelson, Inc. Used by permission.

Holy Bible, New Living Translation, (NLT) copyright © 1996. Used by permission of Tyndale House Publishers, Inc., Wheaton, Illinois 60189. All rights reserved.

The Message (MSG)- This edition issued by contractual arrangement with NavPress, a division of The Navigators, U.S.A. Originally published by NavPress in English as THE MESSAGE: The Bible in Contemporary Language copyright 2002-2003 by Eugene Peterson. All rights reserved.

New Century Version®. (NCV) Copyright © 1987, 1988, 1991 by Word Publishing, a division of Thomas Nelson, Inc. All rights reserved. Used by permission.

The Holy Bible, The Living Bible (TLB), Copyright © 1971 owned by assignment by Illinois Regional Bank N.A. (as trustee). Used by permission of Tyndale House Publishers, Inc., Wheaton, Illinois 60189. All rights reserved.

The New American Standard Bible®, (NASB) Copyright © 1960, 1962, 1963, 1968, 1971, 1972, 1973, 1975, 1977, 1995 by The Lockman Foundation. Used by permission.

The Holman Christian Standard Bible™ (HCSB) Copyright © 1999, 2000, 2001 by Holman Bible Publishers. Used by permission.

Cover Design by Kim Russell / Wahoo Designs
Page Layout by Bart Dawson

ISBN 978-1-60587-376-3

Printed in China

2 3 4 5 6—RRD—17 16 15 14 13

TABLE OF CONTENTS

INTRODUCTION

We know that all things work together
for the good of those who love God:
those who are called according to His purpose.

Romans 8:28 HCSB

I f you're struggling with unexpected circumstances or unwelcome changes, you're not alone. In today's fast-paced world, many people have been caught up in situations that they couldn't predict and still may not fully understand.

God's Word promises that all things work together for the good of those who love Him. Yet sometimes we encounter situations that seem so troubling that we simply cannot comprehend how these events might be a part of God's plan for our lives.

The Christian faith, as communicated through the words of the Holy Bible, is a healing faith. It offers comfort in times of trouble, courage for our fears, hope instead of hopelessness. Through the healing words of God's promises, Christians understand that the Lord continues to manifest His plan in good times and bad.

If you are experiencing the shock of a recent setback, or if you are still mourning a loss from long ago, this book is intended to help. So, during the next 30 days, try this experiment: read one chapter a day and take the ideas in that chapter to heart. Then, apply those lessons to the everyday realities of your life. When you weave God's message into the fabric of your day, you'll quickly discover that God's Word has the power to change everything, including you.

Adversity is not meant to be feared, it is meant to be worked through. If this text assists you, even in a small way, as you move through and beyond your own tough times, it will have served its purpose. May God bless you and keep you, and may He place His hand upon your heart today and forever.

Chapter 1

EMBRACING CHANGE

His message was simple
and austere,
like his desert surroundings:
"Change your life.
God's kingdom is here."

—

Matthew 3:2 MSG

In our fast-paced world, everyday life has become an exercise in managing change. Our circumstances change; our relationships change; our bodies change. We grow older every day, as does our world. Thankfully, God does not change. He is eternal, as are the truths that are found in His Holy Word.

The ideas in this book are intended to help you accept change—and embrace it—as you continue to seek God's unfolding plan for your life.

Are you facing one of life's inevitable "midcourse corrections"? If so, you must place your faith, your trust, and your life in the hands of the One who does not change: your Heavenly Father. He is the unmoving rock upon which you must construct this day and every day. When you do, you are secure.

Trust in the Lord with all your heart, and do not rely on your own understanding; think about Him in all your ways, and He will guide you on the right paths.

Proverbs 3:5-6 HCSB

Let us hold fast the confession of our hope without wavering, for He who promised is faithful.

Hebrews 10:23 NKJV

For we walk by faith, not by sight.

2 Corinthians 5:7 NKJV

The one who understands a matter finds success, and the one who trusts in the Lord will be happy.

Proverbs 16:20 HCSB

For the eyes of the Lord range throughout the earth to show Himself strong for those whose hearts are completely His.

2 Chronicles 16:9 HCSB

ANTICIPATING YOUR NEXT GRAND ADVENTURE

It has been said that a rut is nothing more than a grave with both ends kicked out. That's a thought worth pondering. Have you made your life an exciting adventure, or have you allowed the distractions of everyday life to rob you of a sense of God's purpose?

> With God,
> it isn't who you
> were that matters;
> it's who you are
> becoming.
>
> —
>
> Liz Curtis Higgs

As a Christian, you have every reason to celebrate. So if you find yourself feeling as if you're stuck in a rut, or in an unfortunate circumstance, or in a difficult relationship, abandon the status quo by making the changes that your heart tells you are right. After all, in God's glorious kingdom, there should be no place for disciples who are dejected, discouraged, or disheartened. God has a far better plan than that, and so should you.

In a world kept chaotic by change, you will eventually discover, as I have, that this is one of the most precious qualities of the God we are looking for: He doesn't change.

Bill Hybels

Mere change is not growth. Growth is the synthesis of change and continuity, and where there is no continuity there is no growth.

C. S. Lewis

When I am secure in Christ, I can afford to take a risk in my life. Only the insecure cannot afford to risk failure. The secure can be honest about themselves; they can admit failure; they are able to seek help and try again. They can change.

John Maxwell

A TIP FOR EMBRACING CHANGE

Change is inevitable. Don't fear it. Embrace it.

A MOMENT TO REFLECT

My thoughts about the need to embrace the changes that God has placed along my path.

_____

_____

_____

_____

_____

_____

_____

_____

_____

_____

_____

_____

_____

_____

Chapter 2

GOD DOES NOT CHANGE

*Be still,
and know that I am God.*

—

Psalm 46:10 NKJV

These are times of great uncertainty. As we become accustomed to, and at times almost numbed by, a steady stream of unsettling news, we are reminded that our world is in a state of constant change. But God is not. So when the world seems to be trembling beneath our feet, we can be comforted in the knowledge that our Heavenly Father is the rock that cannot be shaken. His Word promises, "I am the Lord, I do not change" (Malachi 3:6 NKJV).

Every day that we live, we mortals encounter a multitude of changes—some good, some not so good. And on occasion, all of us must endure life-changing personal losses that leave us heartbroken. When we do, our Heavenly Father stands ready to comfort us, to guide us, and—in time—to heal us.

Is the world spinning a little too fast for your liking? Are you facing troubling uncertainties, difficult circumstances, or unwelcome changes? If so, please remember that God is far bigger than any problem you may face. So, instead of worrying about life's inevitable challenges, put your faith in the Father and His only begotten Son. After all, "Jesus Christ is the same yesterday, today, and forever" (Hebrews 13:8 NKJV). And it is precisely because your Savior does not change that you can face your challenges with courage for today and hope for tomorrow.

Are you anxious about situations that you cannot control? Take your anxieties to God. Are you troubled? Take your troubles to Him. Does your little corner of the universe seem to be a frightening place? Seek protection from the One who cannot be moved. The same God who created the universe will protect you if you ask Him . . . so ask Him . . . and then serve Him with willing hands and a trusting heart.

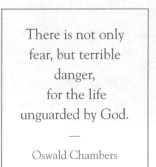

There is not only fear, but terrible danger,
for the life unguarded by God.

—

Oswald Chambers

We know how much God loves us, and we have put our trust in him. God is love, and all who live in love live in God, and God lives in them.

1 John 4:16 NLT

As the Father loved Me, I also have loved you; abide in My love.

John 15:9 NKJV

The unfailing love of the LORD never ends! By his mercies we have been kept from complete destruction.

Lamentations 3:22 NLT

Whoever is wise will observe these things, and they will understand the lovingkindness of the Lord.

Psalm 107:43 NKJV

For God loved the world in this way: He gave His only Son, so that everyone who believes in Him will not perish but have eternal life.

John 3:16 HCSB

Sometimes we need a birds-eye view of what God sees about our lives. If we could just see what he sees we might lighten up a little bit.

Dennis Swanberg

In all the old castles of England, there was a place called the keep. It was always the strongest and best protected place in the castle, and in it were hidden all who were weak and helpless and unable to defend themselves in times of danger. Shall we be afraid to hide ourselves in the keeping power of our Divine Keeper, who neither slumbers nor sleeps, and who has promised to preserve our going out and our coming in, from this time forth and even forever more?

Hannah Whitall Smith

A TIP FOR EMBRACING CHANGE

God is here, and He wants to establish an intimate relationship with you. When you sincerely reach out to Him, you will sense His presence.

A MOMENT TO REFLECT

My thoughts about God's power and His love.

Chapter 3

ACCEPTING THE THINGS YOU CANNOT CHANGE

*For everything created
by God is good, and nothing
should be rejected if it is received
with thanksgiving.*

—

1 Timothy 4:4 HCSB

Are you embittered by an unexpected change or an unwelcome challenge that you did not deserve and cannot understand? If so, it's time to accept the unchangeable past and to have faith in the promise of tomorrow. It's time to trust God completely—and it's time to reclaim the peace—His peace—that can and should be yours.

On occasion, you will be confronted with situations that you simply don't understand. But God does. And He has a reason for everything that He does.

God doesn't explain Himself in ways that we, as mortals with limited insight and clouded vision, can comprehend. So, instead of understanding every aspect of God's unfolding plan for our lives and our universe, we must be satisfied to trust Him completely. We cannot know God's motivations, nor can we understand His actions. We can, however, trust Him, and we must.

A man's heart plans his way, but the Lord determines his steps.

Proverbs 16:9 HCSB

Do not remember the past events, pay no attention to things of old. Look, I am about to do something new; even now it is coming. Do you not see it? Indeed, I will make a way in the wilderness, rivers in the desert.

Isaiah 43:18-19 HCSB

Should we accept only good from God and not adversity?

Job 2:10 HCSB

Come to terms with God and be at peace; in this way good will come to you.

Job 22:21 HCSB

Sheathe your sword! Should I not drink the cup that the Father has given Me?

John 18:11 HCSB

WHEN DREAMS DON'T COME TRUE

Some of our most important dreams are the ones we abandon. Some of our most important goals are the ones we don't attain. Sometimes, our most important journeys are the ones that we take to the winding conclusion of what seem to be dead-end streets. Thankfully, with God there are no dead-ends; there are only opportunities to learn, to yield, to trust, to serve, and to grow.

The next time you experience one of life's inevitable disappointments, don't despair and don't be afraid to try "Plan B." Consider every setback an opportunity to choose a different, more appropriate path. Have faith that God may indeed be leading you in an entirely different direction, a direction of His choosing. And as you take your next step, remember that what looks like a dead-end to you may, in fact, be the fast lane according to God.

Ultimately things
work out best for those
who make the best
of the way things work out.

—

Barbara Johnson

Surrender to the Lord is not a tremendous sacrifice, not an agonizing performance. It is the most sensible thing you can do.

Corrie ten Boom

In the kingdom of God, the surest way to lose something is to try to protect it, and the best way to keep it is to let it go.

A. W. Tozer

Tomorrow's job is fathered by today's acceptance. Acceptance of what, at least for the moment, you cannot alter.

Max Lucado

A TIP FOR EMBRACING CHANGE

Sometimes, the blessings God gives us are not the ones we've asked for. But even when we cannot understand God's plan for our lives, we should be thankful for His eternal perspective and His eternal love.

A MOMENT TO REFLECT

My thoughts about the things I cannot change.

_____

_____

_____

_____

_____

_____

_____

_____

_____

_____

_____

_____

_____

_____

Chapter 4

GOD'S PLAN AND YOUR TOUGH TIMES

Who are those who fear the Lord?
He will show them the path
they should choose.
They will live in prosperity,
and their children
will inherit the Promised Land.

—

Psalm 25:12-13 NLT

I t's an age-old riddle: Why does God allow us to endure tough times? After all, since we trust that God is all-powerful, and since we trust that His hand shapes our lives, why doesn't He simply rescue us—and our loved ones—from all hardship and pain?

God's Word teaches us again and again that He loves us and wants the best for us. And the Bible also teaches us that God is ever-present and always watchful. So why, we wonder, if God is really so concerned with every detail of our lives, does He permit us to endure emotions like grief, sadness, shame, or fear? And why does He allow tragic circumstances to invade the lives of good people? These questions perplex us, especially when times are tough.

On occasion, all of us face adversity, and throughout life, we all must endure life-changing personal losses that leave us breathless. When we pass through the dark valleys of life, we often ask, "Why me?" Sometimes, of course, the answer is obvious—sometimes we make mistakes, and we must pay for them. But on other occasions, when we have done nothing wrong, we wonder why God allows us to suffer.

Even when we cannot understand God's plans, we must trust them. And even when we are impatient for our situations to improve, we must trust God's timing. If we seek to live in accordance with His plan for our lives, we must continue to study His Word (in good times and bad), and we must be watchful for His signs, knowing that in time, He will lead us through the valleys, onward to the mountaintop.

> *It is God who works in you to will and to act according to his good purpose.*
>
> —
>
> Philippians 2:13 NIV

So if you're enduring tough times, don't give up and don't give in. God still has glorious plans for you. So keep your eyes and ears open . . . as well as your heart.

"For I know the plans I have for you," declares the Lord, "plans to prosper you and not to harm you, plans to give you hope and a future. Then you will call upon me and come and pray to me, and I will listen to you."

Jeremiah 29:11-12 NIV

And we know that in all things God works for the good of those who love him, who have been called according to his purpose.

Romans 8:28 NIV

He replied, "Every plant that My heavenly Father didn't plant will be uprooted."

Matthew 15:13 HCSB

The steps of the Godly are directed by the Lord. He delights in every detail of their lives. Though they stumble, they will not fall, for the Lord holds them by the hand.

Psalm 37:23-24 NLT

FINDING NEW MEANING

Perhaps tough times have turned your world upside down. Maybe it seems to you as if everything in your life has been rearranged. Or perhaps your relationships and your responsibilities have been permanently altered. If so, you may come face to face with the daunting task of finding new purpose for your life. And God is willing to help.

God has an important plan for your life, and part of His plan may well be related to the tough times you're experiencing. After all, you've learned important, albeit hard-earned, lessons. And you're certainly wiser today than you were yesterday. So your suffering carries with it great potential: the potential for intense personal growth and the potential to help others.

As you begin to reorganize your life, look for ways to use your experiences for the betterment of others. When you do, you can rest assured that the course of your recovery will depend upon how quickly you discover new people to help and new reasons to live. And as you move through and beyond your own particular tough times, be mindful of this fact: as a survivor, you will have countless opportunities to serve others. By serving others, you will bring glory to God and meaning to the hardships you've endured.

On the darkest day of your life,
God is still in charge.
Take comfort in that.

—

Marie T. Freeman

Our loving God uses difficulty in our lives to burn away the sin of self and build faith and spiritual power.

Bill Bright

Don't let circumstances distress you. Rather, look for the will of God for your life to be revealed in and through those circumstances.

Billy Graham

A TIP FOR EMBRACING CHANGE

Sometimes, waiting faithfully for God's plan to unfold is more important than understanding God's plan. Ruth Bell Graham once said, "When I am dealing with an all-powerful, all-knowing God, I, as a mere mortal, must offer my petitions not only with persistence, but also with patience. Someday I'll know why." So, even when you can't understand God's plans, you must trust Him and never lose faith!

A MOMENT TO REFLECT

My thoughts about the importance of cultivating a positive self-image.

_____

_____

_____

_____

_____

_____

_____

_____

_____

_____

_____

_____

_____

Chapter 5

MANAGING STRESS

*The peace of God,
which surpasses
all understanding,
will guard your hearts
and minds through Christ Jesus.*

—

Philippians 4:7 NKJV

Stressful days are an inevitable fact of modern life. And how do we best cope with the challenges of our demanding, 21st-century world? By turning our days and our lives over to God. Elisabeth Elliot writes, "If my life is surrendered to God, all is well. Let me not grab it back, as though it were in peril in His hand but would be safer in mine!" Yet even the most devout Christian may, at times, seek to grab the reins of her life and proclaim, "I'm in charge!" To do so is foolish, prideful, and stressful.

When we seek to impose our own wills upon the world—or upon other people—we invite stress into our lives . . . needlessly. But, when we turn our lives and our hearts over to God—when we accept His will instead of seeking vainly to impose our own—we discover the inner peace that can be ours through Him.

Do you feel overwhelmed by the stresses of daily life? Turn your concerns and your prayers over to God. Trust Him. Trust Him completely. Trust Him today. Trust Him always. When it comes to the inevitable challenges of this day, hand them over to God completely and without reservation. He knows your needs and will meet those needs in His own way and in His own time if you let Him.

LORD, help! they cried in their trouble, and he saved them from their distress.

Psalm 107:13 NLT

You have allowed me to suffer much hardship, but you will restore me to life again and lift me up from the depths of the earth. You will restore me to even greater honor and comfort me once again.

Psalm 71:20-21 NLT

When my heart is overwhelmed: lead me to the rock that is higher than I.

Psalm 61:2 KJV

God, who comforts the downcast, comforted us.

2 Corinthians 7:6 NIV

SLOWING DOWN
THE MERRY-GO-ROUND

Every major change, whether bad or good, puts stress on you and your family. That's why it's sensible to plan things so that you don't invite too many changes into your life at once. Of course, you'll be tempted to do otherwise. Once you land that new job, you'll be sorely tempted to buy the new house and the new car. Or if you've just gotten married, you'll be tempted to buy everything in sight—while the credit card payments mount. Don't do it!

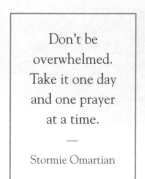

Don't be overwhelmed. Take it one day and one prayer at a time.

—

Stormie Omartian

When it comes to making big changes or big purchases, proceed slowly. Otherwise, you may find yourself uncomfortably perched atop a merry-go-round that is much easier to start than it is to stop.

The better acquainted you become with God, the less tensions you feel and the more peace you possess.

Charles Allen

When frustrations develop into problems that stress you out, the best way to cope is to stop, catch your breath, and do something for yourself, not out of selfishness, but out of wisdom.

Barbara Johnson

Satan does some of his worst work on exhausted Christians when nerves are frayed and the mind is faint.

Vance Havner

A TIP FOR EMBRACING CHANGE

If you're experiencing too much stress, you should make sure that you're not neglecting your prayer life. Prayer is a powerful tool for managing stress, so pray often and early.

A MOMENT TO REFLECT

My thoughts about some common-sense ways that I can manage stress.

_____

_____

_____

_____

_____

_____

_____

_____

_____

_____

_____

_____

_____

_____

Chapter 6

SELF-ESTEEM ACCORDING TO GOD

*For you made us only
a little lower than God,
and you crowned us
with glory and honor.*

—

Psalm 8:5 NLT

When you experience life-altering changes, you may lose self-confidence. Or you may become so focused on what other people are thinking—or saying—that you fail to focus on God. To do so is a mistake of major proportions—don't make it. Instead, seek God's guidance as you focus your energies on becoming the best you that you can possibly be. And when it comes to matters of self-esteem and self-image, seek approval not from your peers, but from God.

Millions of words have been written about various ways to improve self-image and increase self-esteem. Yet, maintaining a healthy self-image is, to a surprising extent, a matter of doing three things: 1. Obeying God 2. Thinking healthy thoughts. 3. Finding a purpose for your life that pleases your Creator and yourself.

The following common-sense, Biblically-based tips can help you build the kind of self-image—and the kind of life—that both you and God can be proud of:

1. Do the right thing: If you're misbehaving, how can you possibly hope to feel good about yourself? (Romans 14:12)

2. Watch what you think: If your inner voice is, in reality, your inner critic, you need to tone down the criticism now. And while you're at it, train yourself to begin thinking thoughts that are more rational, more accepting, and less judgmental. (Philippians 4:8)

3. Spend time with boosters, not critics: Are your friends putting you down? If so, find new friends. (Hebrews 3:13)

4. Don't be a perfectionist: Strive for excellence, but never confuse it with perfection. (Ecclesiastes 11:4,6)

5. If you're addicted to something unhealthy, stop; if you can't stop, get help. Addictions, of whatever type, create havoc in your life. And disorder. And grief. And low self-esteem. (Exodus 20:3)

6. Find a purpose for your life that is larger than you are: When you're dedicated to something or someone besides yourself, you blossom. (Ephesians 6:7)

7. Don't worry too much about self-esteem: Instead, worry more about living a life that is pleasing to God. Learn to think optimistically. Find a worthy purpose. Find people to love and people to serve. When you do, your self-esteem will, on most days, take care of itself.

You're blessed when you're content with just who you are—no more, no less. That's the moment you find yourselves proud owners of everything that can't be bought.

Matthew 5:5 MSG

A devout life does bring wealth, but it's the rich simplicity of being yourself before God.

1 Timothy 6:6 MSG

To acquire wisdom is to love oneself; people who cherish understanding will prosper.

Proverbs 19:8 NLT

TRUST GOD AND START FIXING
WHAT'S BROKEN

When life unfolds according to our wishes, or when we experience unexpected good fortune, we find it easy to praise God's plan. That's when we greet change with open arms. But sometimes the changes that we must endure are painful. When we struggle through the difficult days of life, as we must from time to time, we may ask ourselves, "Why me?" The answer, of course, is that God knows, but He isn't telling . . . yet.

> Comparison is the root of all feelings of inferiority.
>
> —
>
> James Dobson

Have you endured a difficult transition that has left your head spinning or your heart broken? If so, you have a clear choice to make: either you can cry and complain, or you can trust God and get busy fixing what's broken. The former is a formula for disaster; the latter is a formula for a well-lived life.

As you and I lay up for ourselves living, lasting treasures in Heaven, we come to the awesome conclusion that we ourselves are His treasure!

Anne Graham Lotz

The Creator has made us each one of a kind. There is nobody else exactly like us, and there never will be. Each of us is his special creation and is alive for a distinctive purpose.

Luci Swindoll

By the grace of God you are what you are; glory in your selfhood, accept yourself and go on from there.

Wilferd Peterson

A TIP FOR EMBRACING CHANGE

Don't make the mistake of selling yourself short. No matter the size of your challenges, you can be sure that you and God, working together, can tackle them.

A MOMENT TO REFLECT

My thoughts about constructive things I can do to manage stress.

_____

_____

_____

_____

_____

_____

_____

_____

_____

_____

_____

_____

_____

_____

Chapter 7

A RENEWED SENSE OF PURPOSE

You will show me the way of life,
granting me the joy
of your presence
and the pleasures of living
with you forever.

—

Psalm 16:11 NLT

I f you're experiencing unexpected changes, you may be asking yourself, "What does God want me to do next?" Perhaps you're pondering your future, uncertain of your plans, unsure of your next step. But even if you don't have a clear plan for the next step of your life's journey, you may rest assured that God does.

God has a plan for the universe, and He has a plan for you. He understands that plan as thoroughly and completely as He knows you. If you seek God's will earnestly and prayerfully, He will make His plans known to you in His own time and in His own way.

Do you sincerely want to discover God's purpose for your life? If so, you must first be willing to live in accordance with His commandments. You must also study God's Word and be watchful for His signs. Finally, you should open yourself up to the Creator every day—beginning with this one—and you must have faith that He will soon reveal His plans to you.

Perhaps your vision of God's purpose for your life has been clouded by a wish list that you have expected God to dutifully fulfill. Perhaps you have fervently hoped that God would create a world that unfolds according to your wishes, not His. If so, you have probably experienced more disappointment than satisfaction and more frustration than peace. A better strategy is to conform your will to God's (and not to struggle vainly in an attempt to conform His will to yours).

God's plans and purposes may sometimes seem unmistakably clear to you. If so, push ahead. But other times, He may lead you through the wilderness before He directs you to the Promised Land. So be patient and keep seeking His will for your life. When you do, you'll be amazed at the marvelous things that an all-powerful, all-knowing God can do.

Some virtues cannot be produced in us without affliction.

—

C. H. Spurgeon

Whatever you do, do all to the glory of God.

1 Corinthians 10:31 NKJV

You're sons of Light, daughters of Day. We live under wide open skies and know where we stand. So let's not sleepwalk through life . . .

1 Thessalonians 5:5-6 MSG

We look at this Son and see the God who cannot be seen. We look at this Son and see God's original purpose in everything created.

Colossians 1:15 MSG

To everything there is a season, a time for every purpose under heaven.

Ecclesiastes 3:1 NKJV

There is one thing I always do. Forgetting the past and straining toward what is ahead, I keep trying to reach the goal and get the prize for which God called me . . .

Philippians 3:13-14 NCV

God will make obstacles serve His purpose.

Mrs. Charles E. Cowman

When we realize and embrace the Lord's will for us, we will love to do it. We won't want to do anything else. It's a passion.

Franklin Graham

Whatever clouds you face today, ask Jesus, the light of the world, to help you look behind the cloud to see His glory and His plans for you.

Billy Graham

A TIP FOR EMBRACING CHANGE

Perhaps you're in a hurry to understand God's unfolding plan for your life. If so, remember that God operates according to a perfect timetable. That timetable is His, not yours. So be patient. God may have quite a few lessons to teach you before you are fully prepared to do His will and fulfill His purpose.

A MOMENT TO REFLECT

My thoughts about the importance of discovering (or rediscovering, if necessary) God's unfolding purpose for my life.

_____

_____

_____

_____

_____

_____

_____

_____

_____

_____

_____

_____

_____

_____

Chapter 8

EVEN WHEN CHANGE IS DIFFICULT, NO PROBLEMS ARE TOO BIG FOR GOD

Is anything too hard for the LORD?

—

Genesis 18:14 KJV

Here's a riddle: What is it that is too unimportant to pray about yet too big for God to handle? The answer, of course, is: "nothing." Yet sometimes, when the challenges of the day seem overwhelming, we may spend more time worrying about our troubles than praying about them. And, we may spend more time fretting about our problems than solving them. A far better strategy, of course, is to pray as if everything depended entirely upon God and to work as if everything depended entirely upon us.

Life is an exercise in problem-solving. The question is not whether we will encounter problems; the real question is how we will choose to address them. When it comes to solving the problems of everyday living, we often know precisely what needs to be done, but we may be slow in doing it—especially if what needs to be done is difficult or uncomfortable for us. So we put off till tomorrow what should be done today.

The words of Psalm 34 remind us that the Lord solves problems for "people who do what is right." And usually, "doing what is right" means doing the uncomfortable work of confronting our problems sooner rather than later. So with no further ado, let the problem-solving begin . . . now!

People who do what is right may have many problems, but the Lord will solve them all.

Psalm 34:19 NCV

For when the way is rough, your patience has a chance to grow. So let it grow, and don't try to squirm out of your problems.

James 1:3-4 TLB

When you go through deep waters and great trouble, I will be with you. When you go through the rivers of difficulty, you will not drown! When you walk through the fire of oppression, you will not be burned up; the flames will not consume you. For I am the Lord, your God . . .

Isaiah 43:2-3 NLT

DO SOMETHING TODAY

Perhaps your troubles are simply too big to solve in a single sitting. But just because you can't solve everything doesn't mean that you should do nothing. So today, as a favor to yourself and as a way of breaking the bonds of procrastination, do something to make your situation better. Even a small step in the right direction is still a step in the right direction. And a small step is far, far better than no step at all.

Measure the size
of the obstacles against
the size of God.

—

Beth Moore

The grace of God is sufficient for all our needs, for every problem and for every difficulty, for every broken heart, and for every human sorrow.

Peter Marshall

We must face today as children of tomorrow. We must meet the uncertainties of this world with the certainty of the world to come. To the pure in heart nothing really bad can happen . . . not death, but sin, should be our greatest fear.

A. W. Tozer

Troubles we bear trustfully can bring us a fresh vision of God and a new outlook on life, an outlook of peace and hope.

Billy Graham

A TIP FOR EMBRACING CHANGE

When it comes to solving problems, work beats worry. Remember: it is better to fix than to fret.

A MOMENT TO REFLECT

My thoughts about an important challenge I
need to address today.

_____

_____

_____

_____

_____

_____

_____

_____

_____

_____

_____

_____

_____

Chapter 9

ENDURING THE LOSS OF EMPLOYMENT

You are my hope; O Lord GOD,
You are my confidence.

—

Psalm 71:5 NASB

Whether we like it or not, we live in a highly competitive global economy. And whether we like it or not, our jobs, like the ever-changing world in which we live, are in a constant state of flux.

Losing one's job can be a traumatic experience. Job loss is usually a problem of the first magnitude, a problem that results in financial and emotional stress. But of this we can be certain: hidden beneath every problem is the seed of a solution—God's solution. Our challenge, as faithful believers, is to trust God's providence and seek His solutions. When we do, we eventually discover that God does nothing without a very good reason: His reason.

> I will give you
> a new heart and
> put a new spirit
> within you.
>
> —
>
> Ezekiel 36:26 HCSB

If you've recently experienced a job loss, here are some things to consider and some things to do:

1. Remember that God is still here: He rules the mountaintops of life and the valleys, so don't lose hope. (Lamentations 3:25-26)

2. If you're feeling sorry for yourself, stop: Self-pity isn't going to help you find a better job or build a better life. (2 Timothy 1:7)

3. If you're out of a job, you have a critically important job: finding a new one. Don't delay; don't take an extended vacation; don't try to improve your golf game; don't watch daytime TV. If you need a new job, you should spend at least 40 hours a week looking for it. And you should keep doing so until you find the job you need. (1 Chronicles 28:20)

4. Use all available tools. Those tools include, but are not limited to, friends, family, church members, former business associates, classified advertisements, employment services, the Internet, and your own shoe leather. (2 Peter 1:5-6)

5. Think positive thoughts. Think positively about yourself, your abilities, and your future. After all, if you don't believe in those things, how can you expect your future employer to believe in them, either? (Philippians 4:8)

Then the One seated on the throne said, "Look! I am making everything new."

Revelation 21:5 HCSB

But those who wait on the Lord shall renew their strength; they shall mount up with wings like eagles, they shall run and not be weary, they shall walk and not faint.

Isaiah 40:31 NKJV

Therefore if anyone is in Christ, he is a new creature; the old things passed away; behold, new things have come.

2 Corinthians 5:17 HCSB

You are being renewed in the spirit of your minds; you put on the new man, the one created according to God's likeness in righteousness and purity of the truth.

Ephesians 4:23-24 HCSB

If we indulge in any confidence that is not grounded on the Rock of Ages, our confidence is worse than a dream, it will fall on us and cover us with its ruins, causing sorrow and confusion.

C. H. Spurgeon

God's omniscience can instill you with a supernatural confidence that can transform your life.

Bill Hybels

I'm convinced that there is nothing that can happen to me in this life that is not precisely designed by a sovereign Lord to give me the opportunity to learn to know Him.

Elisabeth Elliot

A TIP FOR EMBRACING CHANGE

Keep looking until you find a job that is a good match for your particular skills. That job is out there . . . it's up to you to find it.

A MOMENT TO REFLECT

My thoughts about the career that's best for me.

_____

_____

_____

_____

_____

_____

_____

_____

_____

_____

_____

_____

_____

Chapter 10

RENEWED DAY BY DAY

Every morning he wakes me.
He teaches me
to listen like a student.
The Lord God helps me learn…

—

Isaiah 50:4-5 NCV

E ach new day is a gift from God, and if you are wise, you will spend a few quiet moments each morning thanking the Giver. When you do, you'll discover that time spent with God can lift your spirits and relieve your stress.

Warren Wiersbe writes, "Surrender your mind to the Lord at the beginning of each day." And that's sound advice. When you begin each day with your head bowed and your heart lifted, you are reminded of God's love, His protection, and His commandments. Then, you can align your priorities for the coming day with the teachings and commandments that God has placed upon your heart.

So, if you've acquired the unfortunate habit of trying to "squeeze" God into the corners of your life, it's time to reshuffle the items on your to-do list by placing God first. And if you haven't already done so, form the habit of spending quality time with your Father in heaven. He deserves it . . . and so do you.

Teach me Your way, Lord, and I will live by Your truth. Give me an undivided mind to fear Your name.

Psalm 86:11 HCSB

I will instruct you and show you the way to go; with My eye on you, I will give counsel.

Psalm 32:8 HCSB

Happy is the man who finds wisdom, and the man who gains understanding.

Proverbs 3:13 NKJV

But grow in the grace and knowledge of our Lord and Savior Jesus Christ. To Him be the glory both now and to the day of eternity.

2 Peter 3:18 HCSB

In all your ways acknowledge Him, and He shall direct your paths.

Proverbs 3:6 NKJV

PRAY ABOUT IT

Andrew Murray observed, "Some people pray just to pray, and some people pray to know God." Your task, as a maturing believer, is to pray, not out of habit or obligation, but out of a sincere desire to know your Heavenly Father. Through constant prayers, you should petition God, you should praise Him, and you should seek to discover His unfolding plans for your life.

> A person with no devotional life generally struggles with faith and obedience.
>
> —
>
> Charles Stanley

Today, reach out to the Giver of all blessings. Turn to Him for guidance and for strength. Invite Him into every corner of your day. Ask Him to teach you and to lead you. And remember that no matter your circumstances, God is never far away; He is here . . . always right here. So pray.

Every morning God gives us the gift of comprehending anew His faithfulness of old; thus in the midst of our life with God, we may daily begin a new life with Him.

Dietrich Bonhoeffer

Think of this—we may live together with Him here and now, a daily walking with Him who loved us and gave Himself for us.

Elisabeth Elliot

Jesus challenges you and me to keep our focus daily on the cross of His will if we want to be His disciples.

Anne Graham Lotz

A TIP FOR EMBRACING CHANGE

Make a promise to yourself and keep it that you will begin each day with a morning devotional. A regular time of quiet reflection and prayer will allow you to praise your Creator and to focus your thoughts. A daily devotional is especially important during those times of your life when you're feelings discouraged, fearful, or stressed.

A MOMENT TO REFLECT

My thoughts about the importance of spending time with God every morning.

_____

_____

_____

_____

_____

_____

_____

_____

_____

_____

_____

_____

_____

Chapter 11

THE RIGHT KIND OF ATTITUDE

For God has not given us a spirit of fearfulness, but one of power, love, and sound judgment.

—

2 Timothy 1:7 HCSB

If you want to build a better future for yourself and your family, you need the right kind of attitude: the positive kind. So what's your attitude today? Are you fearful, angry, bored, or worried? Are you pessimistic, perplexed, pained, and perturbed? Are you moping around with a frown on your face that's almost as big as the one in your heart? If so, God wants to have a little talk with you.

God created you in His own image, and He wants you to experience joy, contentment, peace, and abundance. But, God will not force you to experience these things; you must claim them for yourself.

God has given you free will, including the ability to influence the direction and the tone of your thoughts. And, here's how God wants you to direct those thoughts:

Finally brothers, whatever is true, whatever is honorable, whatever is just, whatever is pure, whatever is lovely, whatever is commendable—if there is any moral excellence and if there is any praise—dwell on these things (Philippians 4:8 HCSB).

The quality of your attitude will help determine the quality of your life, so you must guard your thoughts accordingly. If you make up your mind to approach life with a healthy mixture of realism and optimism, you'll be rewarded. But, if you allow yourself to fall into the unfortunate habit of negative thinking, you will doom yourself to unhappiness, or mediocrity, or worse.

So, the next time you find yourself dwelling upon the negative aspects of your life, refocus your attention on things positive. The next time you find yourself falling prey to the blight of pessimism, stop yourself and turn your thoughts around. The next time you're tempted to waste valuable time gossiping or complaining, resist those temptations with all your might.

And remember: you'll never whine your way to the top . . . so don't waste your breath.

Set your mind on things above, not on things on the earth.

Colossians 3:2 NKJV

Come near to God, and God will come near to you. You sinners, clean sin out of your lives. You who are trying to follow God and the world at the same time, make your thinking pure.

James 4:8 NCV

Those who are pure in their thinking are happy, because they will be with God.

Matthew 5:8 NCV

In everything give thanks; for this is the will of God in Christ Jesus for you.

1 Thessalonians 5:18 NKJV

Worship the Lord with gladness. Come before him, singing with joy. Acknowledge that the Lord is God! He made us, and we are his. We are his people, the sheep of his pasture.

Psalm 100:2-3 NLT

FOLLOW HIS LEAD

God promises that He has the power to transform your life if you invite Him to do so. Your decision, then, is straightforward: whether or not to allow the Father's transforming power to work in you and through you.

God stands at the door of your heart and waits; all you must do is to invite Him in. When you do so, you cannot remain unchanged.

Is there some aspect of your life you'd like to change—a bad habit, an unhealthy relationship, or a missed opportunity? Then ask God to change your at-

Your attitude is more important than your aptitude.

—

Zig Ziglar

titude and guide your path. Talk specifically to your Creator about the person you are today and the person you want to become tomorrow. When you sincerely petition the Father, you'll be amazed at the things that He and you, working together, can accomplish.

The mind is like a clock that is constantly running down. It has to be wound up daily with good thoughts.

Fulton J. Sheen

The difference between winning and losing is how we choose to react to disappointment.

Barbara Johnson

It's your choice: you can either count your blessings or recount your disappointments.

Jim Gallery

Pain is inevitable, but misery is optional.

Max Lucado

A TIP FOR EMBRACING CHANGE

A positive attitude leads to positive results; a negative attitude leads elsewhere. And if you want to improve the quality of your thoughts, ask God to help you.

A MOMENT TO REFLECT

My thoughts about the importance of maintaining a positive outlook on my life and my future.

_____

_____

_____

_____

_____

_____

_____

_____

_____

_____

_____

Chapter 12

MAKING PEACE WITH YOUR PAST

*Do not remember the past events,
pay no attention to things of old.
Look, I am about to do
something new;
even now it is coming.
Do you not see it? Indeed, I will
make a way in the wilderness,
rivers in the desert.*

—

Isaiah 43:18-19 HCSB

The American theologian Reinhold Niebuhr composed a profoundly simple verse that came to be known as the Serenity Prayer: "God, grant me the serenity to accept the things I cannot change, the courage to change the things I can, and the wisdom to know the difference." Niebuhr's words are far easier to recite than they are to live by. Why? Because most of us want life to unfold in accordance with our own wishes and timetables. But sometimes God has other plans.

One of the things that fits nicely into the category of "things we cannot change" is the past. Yet even though we know that the past is unchangeable, many of us continue to invest energy worrying about the unfairness of yesterday (when we should, instead, be focusing on the opportunities of today and the promises of tomorrow). Author Hannah Whitall Smith observed, "How changed our lives would be if

The pages of your past cannot be rewritten, but the pages of your tomorrows are blank.

—

Zig Ziglar

we could only fly through the days on wings of surrender and trust!" These words remind us that, even when we cannot understand the past, we must trust God and accept His will.

So, if you've endured a difficult past, accept it and learn from it, but don't spend too much time here in the precious present fretting over memories of the unchangeable past. Instead, trust God's plan and look to the future. After all, the future is where everything that's going to happen to you from this moment on is going to take place.

*I have learned,
in whatsoever state I am,
therewith to be content.*

—

Philippians 4:11 KJV

All bitterness, anger and wrath, insult and slander must be removed from you, along with all wickedness. And be kind and compassionate to one another, forgiving one another, just as God also forgave you in Christ.

Ephesians 4:31-32 HCSB

Should we accept only good from God and not adversity?

Job 2:10 HCSB

Brothers, I do not consider myself to have taken hold of it. But one thing I do: forgetting what is behind and reaching forward to what is ahead, I pursue as my goal the prize promised by God's heavenly call in Christ Jesus.

Philippians 3:13-14 HCSB

For if you forgive people their wrongdoing, your heavenly Father will forgive you as well. But if you don't forgive people, your Father will not forgive your wrongdoing.

Matthew 6:14-15 HCSB

ACCEPTING THE PAST, LIVING IN THE PRESENT

Manmade plans are fallible; God's plans are not. Yet whenever life takes an unexpected turn, we are tempted to fall into the spiritual traps of worry, self-pity, or bitterness. God intends that we do otherwise.

The old saying is familiar: "Forgive and forget." But when we have been hurt badly, forgiveness is often difficult and forgetting is downright impossible. Since we can't forget yesterday's troubles, we should learn from them. Yesterday has much to teach us about tomorrow. We may learn from the past, but we should never live in the past. God has given each of us a glorious day: this one. And it's up to each of us to use this day as faithful stewards, not as embittered historians.

So if you're trying to forget the past, don't waste your time. Instead, try a different approach: learn to accept the past and live in the present. Then, you can focus your thoughts and your energies, not on the struggles of yesterday, but instead on the profound opportunities that God has placed before you today.

We need to be at peace with our past, content with our present, and sure about our future, knowing they are all in God's hands.

Joyce Meyer

Leave the broken, irreversible past in God's hands, and step out into the invincible future with Him.

Oswald Chambers

Not the power to remember, but its very opposite, the power to forget, is a necessary condition for our existence.

St. Basil

A TIP FOR EMBRACING CHANGE

The past is past, so don't invest all your energy there. If you're focused on the past, change your focus. If you're living in the past, move on.

A MOMENT TO REFLECT

My thoughts about the rewards of focusing on the present, not the past.

_____

_____

_____

_____

_____

_____

_____

_____

_____

_____

_____

_____

_____

Chapter 13

DON'T GIVE UP!

*No matter how many times you
trip them up, God-loyal people
don't stay down long;
Soon they're up on their feet,
while the wicked end up flat
on their faces.*

—

Proverbs 24:16 MSG

The old saying is as true today as it was when it was first spoken: "Life is a marathon, not a sprint." That's why wise travelers (like you) select a traveling companion who never tires and never falters. That partner, of course, is your Heavenly Father.

The next time you find your courage tested by an unwelcome change, remember that God is as near as your next breath, and remember that He offers strength and comfort to His children. He is your shield and your strength; He is your protector and your deliverer. Call upon Him in your hour of need and then be comforted. Whatever your challenge, whatever your trouble, God can help you persevere. And that's precisely what He'll do if you ask Him.

Perhaps you are in a hurry for God to help you resolve your challenges. Perhaps you're anxious to earn the rewards that you feel you've already earned from life. Perhaps you're drumming your fingers, impatiently waiting for God to act. If so, be forewarned: God operates on His own timetable, not yours. Sometimes, God may answer your prayers with silence, and when He does, you must patiently persevere. In times of trouble, you must remain steadfast and trust in the merciful goodness of your Heavenly Father. Whatever your problem, He can handle it. Your job is to keep persevering until He does.

Let us not become weary in doing good, for at the proper time we will reap a harvest if we do not give up.

Galatians 6:9 NIV

For you have need of endurance, so that when you have done the will of God, you may receive what was promised.

Hebrews 10:36 NASB

Thanks be to God! He gives us the victory through our Lord Jesus Christ. Therefore, my dear brothers, stand firm. Let nothing move you. Always give yourselves fully to the work of the Lord, because you know that your labor in the Lord is not in vain.

1 Corinthians 15:57-58 NIV

LOOK TO JESUS

In a world filled with roadblocks and stumbling blocks, we need strength, courage, and perseverance. And, as an example of perfect perseverance, we need look no further than our Savior, Jesus Christ.

Jesus finished what He began. Despite the torture He endured, despite the shame of the cross, Jesus was steadfast in His faithfulness to God. We, too, must remain faithful, especially during times of hardship.

As you navigate the inevitable changes of modern-day life, you will undoubtedly experience your fair share of disappointments, detours, false starts, and failures. When you do, don't become discouraged: God's not finished with you yet.

> We don't give up.
> We look up.
> We trust. We believe.
> And our optimism
> is not hollow.
> Christ has proven
> worthy. He has
> shown that he never
> fails. That's what
> makes God, God.
>
> —
>
> Max Lucado

The sermon of your life in tough times ministers to people more powerfully than the most eloquent speaker.

Bill Bright

Failure is one of life's most powerful teachers. How we handle our failures determines whether we're going to simply "get by" in life or "press on."

Beth Moore

Just remember, every flower that ever bloomed had to go through a whole lot of dirt to get there!

Barbara Johnson

A TIP FOR EMBRACING CHANGE

If things don't work out at first, don't quit. If you don't keep trying, you'll never know how good you can be.

A MOMENT TO REFLECT

My thoughts about the power of perseverance.

Chapter 14

CONSIDER
THE
POSSIBILITIES

*For nothing will be impossible
with God.*

—

Luke 1:37 HCSB

As you think about ways to manage change and embrace it, don't put limitations on God. He has the power to do miraculous things with you and through you . . . if you let Him.

Are you afraid to ask God to do big things—or to make big changes—in your life? Is your faith threadbare and worn? If so, it's time to abandon your doubts and reclaim your faith in God's promises.

Ours is a God of infinite possibilities. But sometimes, because of limited faith and limited understanding, we wrongly assume that God cannot or will not intervene in the affairs of mankind. Such assumptions are simply wrong.

God's Holy Word makes it clear: absolutely nothing is impossible for the Lord. And since the Bible means what it says, you can be comforted in the knowledge that the Creator of the universe can do miraculous things in your own life and in the lives of your loved ones. Your challenge, as a believer, is to take God at His word and to expect the miraculous.

Let us not lose heart in doing good, for in due time we shall reap if we do not grow weary. So then, while we have opportunity, let us do good to all men, and especially to those who are of the household of the faith.

Galatians 6:9-10 NASB

Make the most of every opportunity.

Colossians 4:5 NIV

God is our refuge and strength, a helper who is always found in times of trouble.

Psalm 46:1 HCSB

Dear brothers and sisters, whenever trouble comes your way, let it be an opportunity for joy. For when your faith is tested, your endurance has a chance to grow. So let it grow, for when your endurance is fully developed, you will be strong in character and ready for anything.

James 1:2-4 NLT

OPPORTUNITIES EVERYWHERE

As you look at the landscape of your life, do you see opportunities, possibilities, and blessings, or do you focus, instead, upon the more negative scenery? Do you spend more time counting your blessings or your misfortunes? If you've acquired the unfortunate habit of focusing too intently upon the negative aspects of life, then your spiritual vision is in need of correction.

Whether you realize it or not, opportunities are whirling around you like stars crossing the night sky: beautiful to observe, but too numerous to count. Yet you may be too concerned with the challenges of everyday living to notice those opportunities. That's why you should slow down occasionally, catch your breath, and focus your thoughts on two things: the talents God has given you and the opportunities that He has placed before you. God is leading you in the direction of those opportunities. Your task is to watch carefully, to pray fervently, and to act accordingly.

Man's adversity is God's opportunity.

Matthew Henry

Often God shuts a door in our face so that he can open the door through which he wants us to go.

Catherine Marshall

God specializes in taking tragedy and turning it into triumph. The greater the tragedy, the greater the potential for triumph.

Charles Stanley

A TIP FOR EMBRACING CHANGE

Focus on possibilities, not roadblocks. The road of life contains a number of potholes and stumbling blocks. Of course you will encounter them from time to time, and so will your family members. But, don't invest large quantities of your life focusing on past misfortunes. On the road of life, regret is a dead end.

A MOMENT TO REFLECT

My thoughts about the miraculous things God has done in the past, and the miraculous things He can do today.

_____

_____

_____

_____

_____

_____

_____

_____

_____

_____

_____

Chapter 15

WHEN DEPRESSION HITS

Weeping may go on all night,
but joy comes with the morning.

—

Psalm 30:5 NLT

Throughout our lives, all of us must endure personal losses that leave us struggling to find hope. The sadness that accompanies such losses is an inescapable fact of life—but in time, we move beyond our grief as the sadness runs its course and life returns to normal. Depression, however, is more than sadness . . . much more.

Depression is a physical and emotional condition that is, in almost all cases, treatable with medication and counseling. And it is not a disease to be taken lightly. Left untreated, depression presents real dangers to patients' physical health and to their emotional well-being.

If you're feeling blue, perhaps it's a logical response to the disappointments of everyday life. But if your feelings of sadness have lasted longer than you think they should—or if someone close to you fears that your sadness may have evolved into clinical depression—it's time to seek professional help.

> There is no pit so deep that God's love is not deeper still.
>
> —
>
> Corrie ten Boom

Here are a few simple guidelines to consider as you make decisions about possible medical treatment:

1. If your feelings of sadness have resulted in persistent and prolonged changes in sleep patterns, or if you've experience a significant change in weight (either gain or loss), consult your physician.

2. If you have persistent urges toward self-destructive behavior, or if you feel as though you have lost the will to live, consult a professional counselor or physician immediately.

3. If someone you trust urges you to seek counseling, schedule a session with a professionally trained counselor to evaluate your condition.

4. If you are plagued by consistent, prolonged, severe feelings of hopelessness, consult a physician, a professional counselor, or your pastor.

God's Word has much to say about every aspect of your life, including your emotional health. And, when you face concerns of any sort—including symptoms of depression—

remember that God is with you. Your Creator intends that His joy should become your joy. Yet sometimes, amid the inevitable hustle and bustle of daily life, you may forfeit—albeit temporarily—God's joy as you wrestle with the challenges of daily living.

So, if you're feeling genuinely depressed, trust your medical doctor to do his or her part. Then, place your ultimate trust in your benevolent Heavenly Father. His healing touch, like His love, endures forever.

God is a specialist;
He is well able to work
our failures into His plans.
Often the doorway to success is entered
through the hallway of failure.

—

Erwin Lutzer

Now the God of all grace, who called you to His eternal glory in Christ Jesus, will personally restore, establish, strengthen, and support you.

1 Peter 5:10 HCSB

The LORD is my strength and song, and He has become my salvation; He is my God, and I will praise Him . . .

Exodus 15:2 NKJV

Peace, peace to you, and peace to your helpers! For your God helps you.

1 Chronicles 12:18 NKJV

He gives power to the weak, and to those who have no might He increases strength.

Isaiah 40:29 NKJV

I am able to do all things through Him who strengthens me.

Philippians 4:13 HCSB

Feelings of uselessness and hopelessness are not from God, but from the evil one, the devil, who wants to discourage you and thwart your effectiveness for the Lord.

Bill Bright

What the devil loves is that vague cloud of unspecified guilt feeling or unspecified virtue by which he lures us into despair or presumption.

C. S. Lewis

In the soul-searching of our lives, we are to stay quiet so we can hear Him say all that He wants to say to us in our hearts.

Charles Swindoll

A TIP FOR EMBRACING CHANGE

Depression is serious business, and it's a highly treatable disease . . . treat it that way.

A MOMENT TO REFLECT

My thoughts about God's promise to love me and protect me today and forever.

_____

_____

_____

_____

_____

_____

_____

_____

_____

_____

_____

_____

_____

_____

Chapter 16

KEEPING POSSESSIONS IN PERSPECTIVE

*Don't collect for yourselves
treasures on earth, where moth
and rust destroy and where thieves
break in and steal. But collect for
yourselves treasures in heaven,
where neither moth nor rust
destroys, and where thieves
don't break in and steal.
For where your treasure is,
there your heart will be also.*

—

Matthew 6:19-21 HCSB

All too often we focus our thoughts and energies on the accumulation of earthly treasures, creating untold stress in our lives and leaving precious little time to accumulate the only treasures that really matter: the spiritual kind. Our material possessions have the potential to do great good—depending upon how we use them. If we allow the things we own to own us, we may pay dearly for our misplaced priorities.

Society focuses intently on material possessions, but God's Word teaches us time and again that money matters little when compared to the spiritual gifts that the Creator offers to those who put Him first in their lives. So today, keep your possessions in perspective. Remember that God should come first, and everything else next. When you give God His rightful place in your heart, you'll have a clearer vision of the things that really matter. Then, you can joyfully thank your Heavenly Father for spiritual blessings that are, in truth, too numerous to count.

And He told them, "Watch out and be on guard against all greed, because one's life is not in the abundance of his possessions."

Luke 12:15 HCSB

For what does it benefit a man to gain the whole world yet lose his life? What can a man give in exchange for his life?

Mark 8:36-37 HCSB

Anyone trusting in his riches will fall, but the righteous will flourish like foliage.

Proverbs 11:28 HCSB

Put on the whole armor of God, that you may be able to stand against the wiles of the devil.

Ephesians 6:11 NKJV

The Lord knows how to deliver the godly out of temptations.

2 Peter 2:9 NKJV

BEWARE OF BECOMING
TOO FRIENDLY WITH THE WORLD

We live in the world, but we must not worship it. Our duty is to place God first and everything else second. But because we are fallible beings with imperfect faith, placing God in His rightful place is often difficult. In fact, at every turn, or so it seems, we are tempted to do otherwise.

The world is a noisy, distracting place filled with countless opportunities to stray from God's will. The world seems to cry, "Worship me with your time, your money, your energy, and your thoughts!" But God commands otherwise: He commands us to worship Him and Him alone; everything else must be secondary.

> Greed is enslaving. The more you have, the more you want—until eventually avarice consumes you.
>
> —
>
> Kay Arthur

As faithful stewards of what we have, ought we not to give earnest thought to our staggering surplus?

Elisabeth Elliot

It's sobering to contemplate how much time, effort, sacrifice, compromise, and attention we give to acquiring and increasing our supply of something that is totally insignificant in eternity.

Anne Graham Lotz

The Scriptures also reveal warning that if we are consumed with greed, not only do we disobey God, but we will miss the opportunity to allow Him to use us as instruments for others.

Charles Stanley

A TIP FOR EMBRACING CHANGE

God's Word warns against the spiritual trap of materialism. Material possessions may seem appealing at first, but they pale in comparison to the spiritual gifts that God gives to those who put Him first. Count yourself among that number.

A MOMENT TO REFLECT

My thoughts about the dangers of materialism.

_____

_____

_____

_____

_____

_____

_____

_____

_____

_____

_____

_____

_____

_____

Chapter 17

ENDURING TOUGH TIMES

*We also have joy with
our troubles, because we know
that these troubles produce
patience. And patience
produces character, and
character produces hope.*

—

Romans 5:3-4 NCV

As life unfolds, all of us encounter occasional disappointments and setbacks: those occasional visits from Old Man Trouble are simply a fact of life, and none of us are exempt. When tough times arrive, we may be forced to rearrange our plans and our priorities. But even on our darkest days, we must remember that God's love remains constant.

The fact that we encounter adversity is not nearly so important as the way we choose to deal with it. When tough times arrive, we have a clear choice: we can begin the difficult work of tackling our troubles or not. When we summon the courage to look Old Man Trouble squarely in the eye, he usually blinks. But, if we refuse to address our problems, even the smallest annoyances have a way of growing into king-sized catastrophes.

As believers, we know that God loves us and that He will protect us. In times of hardship, He will

> Through all of the crises of life—and we all are going to experience them—we have this magnificent Anchor.
>
> —
>
> Franklin Graham

comfort us; in times of sorrow, He will dry our tears. When we are troubled, or weak, or sorrowful, God is always with us. We must build our lives on the rock that cannot be shaken: we must trust in God. And then, we must get on with the hard work of tackling our problems . . . because if we don't, who will? Or should?

When you pass through the waters,
I will be with you; and through the rivers,
they shall not overflow you.
When you walk through the fire,
you shall not be burned, nor shall
the flame scorch you.
For I am the Lord your God,
The Holy One of Israel, your Savior.

—

Isaiah 43:2-3 NKJV

The LORD also will be a stronghold for the oppressed, a stronghold in times of trouble.

Psalm 9:9 NASB

You pulled me from the brink of death, my feet from the cliff-edge of doom. Now I stroll at leisure with God in the sunlit fields of life.

Psalm 56:13 MSG

Don't fret or worry. Instead of worrying, pray. Let petitions and praises shape your worries into prayers, letting God know your concerns. Before you know it, a sense of God's wholeness, everything coming together for good, will come and settle you down. It's wonderful what happens when Christ displaces worry at the center of your life.

Philippians 4:6-7 MSG

Come to Me, all you who labor and are heavy laden, and I will give you rest. Take My yoke upon you and learn from Me, for I am gentle and lowly in heart, and you will find rest for your souls. For My yoke is easy and My burden is light.

Matthew 11:28-30 NKJV

WHEN YOUR FAITH IS TESTED

Life is a tapestry of good days and difficult days, with good days predominating. During the good days, we are tempted to take our blessings for granted (a temptation that we must resist with all our might). But, during life's difficult days, we discover precisely what we're made of. And more importantly, we discover what our faith is made of.

> Like Paul, we may bear thorns so that we can discover God's perfect sufficiency.
>
> —
>
> Beth Moore

Has your faith been put to the test yet? If so, then you know that with God's help, you can endure life's darker days. But if you have not yet faced the inevitable trials and tragedies of life here on earth, don't worry: you will. And when your faith is put to the test, rest assured that God is perfectly willing—and always ready—to give you strength for the struggle.

It's a good thing to have all the props pulled out from under us occasionally. It gives us some sense of what rock is under our feet, and what is sand. It stops us from taking anything for granted.

Madeleine L'Engle

When we face an impossible situation, all self-reliance and self-confidence must melt away; we must be totally dependent on Him for the resources.

Anne Graham Lotz

If things are tough, remember that every flower that ever bloomed had to go through a whole lot of dirt to get there.

Barbara Johnson

A TIP FOR EMBRACING CHANGE

If you're having tough times, don't hit the panic button and don't keep everything bottled up inside. Find a person you can really trust, and talk things over. A second opinion (or, for that matter, a third, fourth, or fifth opinion) is usually helpful.

A MOMENT TO REFLECT

My thoughts about some the lessons I've learned during tough times.

_____

_____

_____

_____

_____

_____

_____

_____

_____

_____

_____

_____

_____

_____

Chapter 18

DOING IT
TODAY

*If you wait for perfect conditions,
you will never get anything done.*

—

Ecclesiastes 11:4 NLT

When life's inevitable changes seem overwhelming, it's easy (and tempting) to avoid those hard-to-do tasks that you would prefer to avoid altogether. But the habit of procrastination takes a double toll: first, important work goes unfinished, and second, valuable energy is wasted in the process of putting off the things that remain undone.

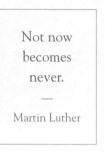

Not now becomes never.

—

Martin Luther

God has created a world that punishes procrastinators and rewards men and women who "do it now." In other words, life doesn't procrastinate. Neither should you. So if you've been putting things off instead of getting things done, here are some things you can do:

1. Have a clear understanding of your short- and long-term goals, and set your priorities in accordance with those goals.

2. When faced with distasteful tasks, do them immediately, preferably first thing in the morning (even if the unpleasantness is a

low-priority activity, go ahead and get it out of the way if it can be completed quickly). Dispatching distasteful tasks sooner rather than later will improve the quality of your day and prevent you from wasting untold amounts of energy in the process of fighting against yourself.

3. Avoid the trap of perfectionism. Be willing to do your best, and be satisfied with the results.

4. If you don't already own one, purchase a daily or weekly planning system that fits your needs. If used properly, a planning calendar is worth many times what you pay for it.

5. Start each work day with a clear written "to-do" list, ranked according to importance. At lunch time, take a moment to collect your thoughts, reexamine your list, and refocus your efforts on the most important things you wish to accomplish during the remainder of the day.

If you do nothing in a difficult time, your strength is limited.

Proverbs 24:10 HCSB

If you are too lazy to plow in the right season, you will have no food at the harvest.

Proverbs 20:4 NLT

When you make a vow to God, do not delay in fulfilling it. He has no pleasure in fools; fulfill your vow.

Ecclesiastes 5:4 NIV

We can't afford to waste a minute, must not squander these precious daylight hours in frivolity and indulgence, in sleeping around and dissipation, in bickering and grabbing everything in sight. Get out of bed and get dressed! Don't loiter and linger, waiting until the very last minute. Dress yourselves in Christ, and be up and about!

Romans 13:13-14 MSG

Whatever you do, do it enthusiastically, as something done for the Lord and not for men.

Colossians 3:23 HCSB

DON'T BE AFRAID TO START SMALL

Perhaps your troubles are simply too big to solve in a single sitting. But just because you can't solve everything doesn't mean that you should do nothing. So today, as a favor to yourself and as a way of breaking the bonds of procrastination, do something to make your situation better. Even a small step in the right direction is still a step in the right direction. And a small step is far, far better than no step at all.

I've found that the worst thing
I can do when it comes to any kind
of potential pressure situation
is to put off dealing with it.

—

John Maxwell

Do the unpleasant work first and enjoy the rest of the day.

Marie T. Freeman

I cannot fix what I will not face.

Jim Gallery

Do not build up obstacles in your imagination. Difficulties must be studied and dealt with, but they must not be magnified by fear.

Norman Vincent Peale

Do noble things, do not dream them all day long.

Charles Kingsley

A TIP FOR EMBRACING CHANGE

The habit of procrastination is often rooted in the fear of failure, the fear of discomfort, or the fear of embarrassment. Your challenge is to confront these fears and defeat them.

A MOMENT TO REFLECT

My thoughts about an important challenge that I've been avoiding.

_____

_____

_____

_____

_____

_____

_____

_____

_____

_____

_____

_____

_____

Chapter 19

LIVE WITH COURAGE

They do not fear bad news;
they confidently trust the Lord
to care for them.
They are confident and fearless
and can face their foes
triumphantly.

—

Psalm 112:7-8 NLT

E very person's life is a tapestry of events: some wonderful, some not-so-wonderful, and some downright disastrous. When we visit the mountaintops of life, praising God isn't hard—in fact, it's easy. In our moments of triumph, we can bow our heads and thank God for our victories. But when we fail to reach the mountaintops, when we endure the inevitable losses that are a part of every person's life, we find it much tougher to give God the praise He deserves. Yet wherever we find ourselves, whether on the mountaintops of life or in life's darkest valleys, we must still offer thanks to God, giving thanks in all circumstances.

The next time you find yourself worried about the challenges of today or the uncertainties of tomorrow, ask yourself this question: are you really ready to place your concerns and your life in God's all-powerful, all-knowing, all-loving hands? If the answer to that question is yes—as it should be—then you can draw courage today from the source of strength that never fails: your Father in heaven.

God is not a distant being. He is not absent from our world, nor is He absent from your world. God is not "out there"; He is "right here," continuously reshaping His universe and continuously reshaping the lives of those who dwell in it.

God is with you always, listening to your thoughts and prayers, watching over your every move. If the demands of everyday life weigh down upon you, you may be tempted to ignore God's presence or—worse yet—to lose faith in His promises. But, when you quiet yourself and acknowledge His presence, God will touch your heart and restore your courage.

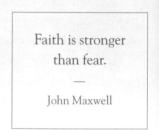

Faith is stronger than fear.

—

John Maxwell

At this very moment—as you're fulfilling your obligations and overcoming tough times—God is seeking to work in you and through you. He's asking you to live abundantly and courageously . . . and He's ready to help. So why not let Him do it . . . starting now?

Be strong and courageous, and do the work. Don't be afraid or discouraged by the size of the task, for the LORD God, my God, is with you. He will not fail you or forsake you.

1 Chronicles 28:20 NLT

Therefore, being always of good courage . . . we walk by faith, not by sight.

2 Corinthians 5:6-7 NASB

God doesn't want us to be shy with his gifts, but bold and loving and sensible.

2 Timothy 1:7 MSG

The LORD himself goes before you and will be with you; he will never leave you nor forsake you. Do not be afraid; do not be discouraged.

Deuteronomy 31:8 NIV

But Moses said to the people, "Do not fear! Stand by and see the salvation of the LORD."

Exodus 14:13 NASB

Faith not only can help you through a crisis, it can help you to approach life after the hard times with a whole new perspective. It can help you adopt an outlook of hope and courage through faith to face reality.

John Maxwell

Seeing that a Pilot steers the ship in which we sail, who will never allow us to perish even in the midst of shipwrecks, there is no reason why our minds should be overwhelmed with fear and overcome with weariness.

John Calvin

Like dynamite, God's power is only latent power until it is released. You can release God's dynamite power into people's lives and into the world through faith, through words, and through prayer.

Bill Bright

Faith is stronger than fear.

John Maxwell

Do not let Satan deceive you into being afraid of God's plans for your life.

R. A. Torrey

Jesus Christ can make the weakest man into a divine dreadnought, fearing nothing.

Oswald Chambers

Perhaps I am stronger than I think.

Thomas Merton

A TIP FOR EMBRACING CHANGE

With God as your partner, you have nothing to fear. Why? Because you and God, working together, can handle absolutely anything that comes your way. So the next time you'd like an extra measure of courage, recommit yourself to a true one-on-one relationship with your Creator. When you sincerely turn to Him, He will never fail you.

A MOMENT TO REFLECT

My thoughts about trusting God to lead me through and beyond today's challenges.

Chapter 20

YOU'RE NEVER ALONE

The Lord is the One
who will go before you.
He will be with you;
He will not leave you
or forsake you.
Do not be afraid or discouraged.

—

Deuteronomy 31:8 HCSB

If God is everywhere, why does He sometimes seem so far away? The answer to that question, of course, has nothing to do with God and everything to do with us.

When we begin each day on our knees, in praise and worship to Him, God often seems very near indeed. But, if we ignore God's presence or—worse yet—rebel against it altogether, the world in which we live becomes a spiritual wasteland.

Are you tired, discouraged or fearful? Be comforted because God is with you. Are you confused or bitter? Talk with God and seek His guidance. Are you celebrating a great victory? Thank God and praise Him. He is the Giver of all things good.

In whatever condition you find yourself, wherever you are, whether you are happy or sad, victorious or vanquished, troubled or triumphant, celebrate God's presence.

> God is in the midst of whatever has happened, is happening, and will happen.
>
> —
>
> Charles Swindoll

Come near to God, and God will come near to you. You sinners, clean sin out of your lives. You who are trying to follow God and the world at the same time, make your thinking pure.

James 4:8 NCV

No, I will not abandon you as orphans—I will come to you.

John 14:18 NLT

Again, this is God's command: to believe in his personally named Son, Jesus Christ. He told us to love each other, in line with the original command. As we keep his commands, we live deeply and surely in him, and he lives in us. And this is how we experience his deep and abiding presence in us: by the Spirit he gave us.

1 John 3:23-24 MSG

For the eyes of the Lord range throughout the earth to strengthen those whose hearts are fully committed to him.

2 Chronicles 16:9 NIV

SPENDING QUIET MOMENTS
WITH GOD

We live in an ever-changing, fast-paced world. The demands of everyday life can seem overwhelming at times, but when we slow ourselves down and seek the presence of a loving God, we invite His peace into our hearts.

Do you set aside quiet moments each day to offer praise to your Creator? You should. During these moments of stillness, you will often sense the infinite love and power of our Lord.

The familiar words of Psalm 46:10 remind us to "be still, and know that I am God." When we do so, we encounter the awesome presence of our loving Heavenly Father, and we are comforted in the knowledge that God is not just near. He is here.

God did this so that men would seek him and perhaps reach out for him and find him, though he is not far from each one of us.

—

Acts 17:27 NIV

God's silence is in no way indicative of His activity or involvement in our lives. He may be silent, but He is not still.

Charles Swindoll

God is not hurried along in the Time-stream of this universe any more than an author is hurried along in the imaginary time of his own novel. He has infinite attention to spare for each one of us. He does not have to deal with us in the mass. You are as much alone with Him as if you were the only being He had ever created. When Christ died, He died for you individually just as much as if you have been the only man in the world.

C. S. Lewis

We should learn to live in the presence of the living God. He should be a well for us: delightful, comforting, unfailing, springing up to eternal life (John 4:14). When we rely on other people, their water supplies ultimately dry up. But, the well of the Creator never fails to nourish us.

C. H. Spurgeon

Certainly, God is with us in times of distress, and that is a comforting truth. But listen: Jesus wants to be part of every experience and every moment of our lives.

Billy Graham

The real test of being in the presence of God is that you either forget about yourself altogether or see yourself as a very small object. It is better to forget about yourself altogether.

C. S. Lewis

Get yourself into the presence of the loving Father. Just place yourself before Him, and look up into, His face; think of His love, His wonderful, tender, pitying love.

Andrew Murray

A TIP FOR EMBRACING CHANGE

Having trouble hearing God? If so, slow yourself down, tune out the distractions, and listen carefully. God has important things to say; your task is to be still and listen.

A MOMENT TO REFLECT

My thoughts about the importance of finding quiet time each day to sense God's presence and His love.

_____

_____

_____

_____

_____

_____

_____

_____

_____

_____

_____

_____

Chapter 21

BE THANKFUL AND WORSHIP HIM

Therefore as you have received Christ Jesus the Lord, walk in Him, rooted and built up in Him and established in the faith, just as you were taught, and overflowing with thankfulness.

—

Colossians 2:6-7 HCSB

As believing Christians, we are blessed beyond measure. God sent His only Son to die for our sins. And, God has given us the priceless gifts of eternal love and eternal life. We, in turn, are instructed to approach our Heavenly Father with reverence and thanksgiving. But sometimes, in the crush of everyday living, we simply don't stop long enough to pause and thank our Creator for the countless blessings He has bestowed upon us.

When we slow down and express our gratitude to the One who made us, we enrich our own lives and the lives of those around us. Thanksgiving should become a habit, a regular part of our daily routines. God has blessed us beyond measure, and we owe Him everything, including our eternal praise.

Praise and thank God for who He is and for what He has done for you.

—

Billy Graham

Are you a thankful person? Do you appreciate the gifts that God has given you? And, do you demonstrate your gratitude by being a faithful steward of the gifts and talents that you have received from your Creator? You most certainly should be thankful. After all, when you stop to think about it, God has given you more blessings than you can count. So the question of the day is this: Will you thank your Heavenly Father . . . or will you spend your time and energy doing other things?

God is always listening—are you willing to say thanks? It's up to you, and the next move is yours.

Thanks be to God for His indescribable gift.

2 Corinthians 9:15 HCSB

And let the peace of the Messiah, to which you were also called in one body, control your hearts. Be thankful.

Colossians 3:15 HCSB

It is good to give thanks to the Lord, and to sing praises to Your name, O Most High.

Psalm 92:1 NKJV

WORSHIP HIM TODAY

God has a wonderful plan for your life, and an important part of that plan includes worship. We should never deceive ourselves: every life is based upon some form of worship. The question is not whether we worship, but what we worship.

Some of us choose to worship God. The result is a plentiful harvest of joy, peace, and abundance. Others distance themselves from God by foolishly worshiping earthly possessions and personal gratification. To do so is a mistake of profound proportions.

Have you accepted the grace of God's only begotten Son? Then worship Him. Worship Him today and every day. Worship Him with sincerity and thanksgiving. Write His name on your heart and rest assured that He, too, has written your name on His.

In everything give thanks; for this is the will of God in Christ Jesus for you.

—

2 Thessalonians 5:18 NKJV

The words "thank" and "think" come from the same root word. If we would think more, we would thank more.

Warren Wiersbe

God often keeps us on the path by guiding us through the counsel of friends and trusted spiritual advisors.

Bill Hybels

The act of thanksgiving is a demonstration of the fact that you are going to trust and believe God.

Kay Arthur

God has promised that if we harvest well with the tools of thanksgiving, there will be seeds for planting in the spring.

Gloria Gaither

A TIP FOR EMBRACING CHANGE

You owe God everything . . . including your thanks.

A MOMENT TO REFLECT

My thoughts about the many ways God has
blessed me and my loved ones.

_____

_____

_____

_____

_____

_____

_____

_____

_____

_____

_____

_____

_____

Chapter 22

STUDY GOD'S WORD

All Scripture is inspired by God and is profitable for teaching, for rebuking, for correcting, for training in righteousness, so that the man of God may be complete, equipped for every good work.

—

2 Timothy 3:16-17 HCSB

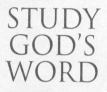

The words of Matthew 4:4 remind us that, "Man shall not live by bread alone but by every word that proceedeth out of the mouth of God" (KJV). As believers, we must study the Bible and meditate upon its meaning for our lives. Otherwise, we deprive ourselves of a priceless gift from our Creator.

God's Word is unlike any other book. The Bible is a road map for life here on earth and for life eternal. As Christians, we are called upon to study God's Holy Word, to follow its commandments, and to share its Good News with the world.

Jonathan Edwards advised, "Be assiduous in reading the Holy Scriptures. This is the fountain whence all knowledge in divinity must be derived. Therefore let not this treasure lie by you neglected." God's Holy Word is, indeed, a priceless, one-of-a-kind treasure, and a passing acquaintance with the Good Book is insufficient for Christians who seek to obey God's Word and to understand His will. After all, man does not live by bread alone . . .

This is my comfort in my affliction, for Your word has given me life.

Psalm 119:50 NKJV

But the word of the Lord endures forever. And this is the word that was preached as the gospel to you.

1 Peter 1:25 HCSB

Let the Word of Christ—the Message—have the run of the house. Give it plenty of room in your lives. Instruct and direct one another using good common sense. And sing, sing your hearts out to God! Let every detail in your lives—words, actions, whatever—be done in the name of the Master, Jesus, thanking God the Father every step of the way.

Colossians 3:16-17 MSG

For the word of God is living and active. Sharper than any double-edged sword, it penetrates even to dividing soul and spirit, joints and marrow; it judges the thoughts and attitudes of the heart.

Hebrews 4:12 NIV

GOD'S WORD REDUCES STRESS

If you're experiencing stress, God's Word can help relieve it. And if you'd like to experience God's peace, Bible study can help provide it.

Warren Wiersbe observed, "When the child of God looks into the Word of God, he sees the Son of God. And, he is transformed by the Spirit of God to share in the glory of God." God's Holy Word is, indeed, life-changing, stress-reducing, one-of-a-kind treasure. And it's up to you—and only you—to use it that way.

The Bible is God's Word,
given to us by God Himself
so we can know Him and His will
for our lives.

—

Billy Graham

God has given us all sorts of counsel and direction in his written Word; thank God, we have it written down in black and white.

John Eldredge

Weave the fabric of God's word through your heart and mind. It will hold strong, even if the rest of life unravels.

Gigi Graham Tchividjian

Nobody ever outgrows Scripture; the book widens and deepens with our years.

C. H. Spurgeon

A TIP FOR EMBRACING CHANGE

If you have a choice to make, the Bible can help you make it. If you've got questions, the Bible has answers. So take a Bible with you wherever you go. You never know when you may need a midday spiritual pick-me-up.

A MOMENT TO REFLECT

My thoughts about the rewards of regular Bible study.

_____

_____

_____

_____

_____

_____

_____

_____

_____

_____

_____

_____

_____

Chapter 23

ACCEPTING ADVICE

A wise man will hear and
increase learning,
and a man of understanding will
attain wise counsel.

—

Proverbs 1:5 NKJV

If you find yourself caught up in a difficult situation, it's time to start searching for knowledgeable friends and mentors who can give you solid advice. Why do you need help evaluating the person in the mirror? Because you're simply too close to that person, that's why. Sometimes, you'll be tempted to give yourself straight As when you deserve considerably lower grades. On other occasions, you'll become your own worst critic, giving yourself a string of failing marks when you deserve better. The truth, of course, is often somewhere in the middle.

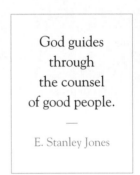

God guides
through
the counsel
of good people.

—

E. Stanley Jones

Finding a wise mentor is only half the battle. It takes just as much wisdom—and sometimes more—to act upon good advice as it does to give it. So find people you can trust, listen to them carefully, and act accordingly.

He is God. Let him do whatever he thinks best.

1 Samuel 3:18 MSG

It is better to be a poor but wise youth than to be an old and foolish king who refuses all advice.

Ecclesiastes 4:13 NLT

It is better to listen to rebuke from a wise person than to listen to the song of fools.

Ecclesiastes 7:5 HCSB

Know-it-alls don't like being told what to do; they avoid the company of wise men and women.

Proverbs 15:12 MSG

Listen to counsel and receive instruction so that you may be wise in later life.

Proverbs 19:20 HCSB

FIND A MENTOR

If you're going through tough times, it's helpful to find mentors who have been there and done that—people who have experienced your particular challenge and lived to tell about it.

When you find mentors who are godly men and women, you become a more godly person yourself. That's why you should seek out advisors who, by their words and their presence, make you a better person and a better Christian.

Today, as a gift to yourself, select, from your friends and family members, a mentor whose judgment you trust. Then listen carefully to your mentor's advice and be willing to accept that advice, even if accepting it requires effort, or pain, or both. Consider your mentor to be God's gift to you. Thank God for that gift, and use it for the glory of His kingdom.

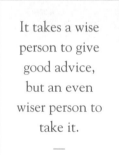

It takes a wise person to give good advice, but an even wiser person to take it.

—

Marie T. Freeman

A single word, if spoken in a friendly spirit, may be sufficient to turn one from dangerous error.

Fanny Crosby

God often keeps us on the path by guiding us through the counsel of friends and trusted spiritual advisors.

Bill Hybels

Do not open your heart to every man, but discuss your affairs with one who is wise and who fears God.

Thomas à Kempis

A TIP FOR EMBRACING CHANGE

If you can't seem to listen to constructive criticism with an open mind, perhaps you've got a severe case of old-fashioned stubbornness. If so, ask God to soften your heart, open your ears, and enlighten your mind.

A MOMENT TO REFLECT

My thoughts about the importance of finding—and listening to—trustworthy mentors.

_____

_____

_____

_____

_____

_____

_____

_____

_____

_____

_____

_____

_____

Chapter 24

USING
YOUR
TALENTS

According to the grace given to
us, we have different gifts:
If prophecy, use it according to
the standard of faith; if service,
in service; if teaching,
in teaching; if exhorting,
in exhortation; giving,
with generosity; leading,
with diligence; showing mercy,
with cheerfulness.

—

Romans 12:6-8 HCSB

God knew precisely what He was doing when He gave you a unique set of talents and opportunities. And now, God wants you to use those talents for the glory of His kingdom. So here's the BIG question: Are you going to use those talents, or not?

Our Heavenly Father instructs us to be faithful stewards of the gifts that He bestows upon us. But we live in a world that encourages us to do otherwise. Ours is a society that is filled to the brim with countless opportunities to squander our time, our resources, and our talents. So we must be watchful for distractions and temptations that might lead us astray.

Every day of your life, you have a choice to make: nurture your talents or neglect them. When you choose wisely, God rewards your efforts, and He expands your opportunities to serve Him.

If you're sincerely interested in building a successful life, build it upon the talents that God (in His infinite wisdom) has given you. Don't try to build a career around the talents you wish He had given you.

In this fast-changing world, God has blessed you with unique opportunities to serve

Him. And, He has given you every tool that you need to do so. Today, accept this challenge: value the talent that God has given you, nourish it, make it grow, and share it with the world. After all, the best way to say "Thank You" for God's gifts is to use them.

His master said to him, "Well done, good and faithful slave! You were faithful over a few things; I will put you in charge of many things. Enter your master's joy!"

Matthew 25:21 HCSB

Every good gift and every perfect gift is from above, and cometh down from the Father of lights.

James 1:17 KJV

Do not neglect the gift that is in you.

1 Timothy 4:14 HCSB

I remind you to keep ablaze the gift of God that is in you.

2 Timothy 1:6 HCSB

BE STILL

Ours is a fast-changing world, a world where the demands of the day can seem overwhelming at times. But, when we slow ourselves down and seek the presence of a loving God, we invite His peace into our hearts.

Do you carve out quiet moments each day to offer thanksgiving and praise to your Creator? You should. During these moments of stillness, you will often sense the infinite love and power of our Lord.

> If you want to reach your potential, you need to add a strong work ethic to your talent.
>
> —
>
> John Maxwell

The familiar words of Psalm 46:10 remind us to "be still, and know that I am God." When we do so, we encounter the awesome presence of our loving Heavenly Father, and we are blessed beyond words.

Employ whatever God has entrusted you with, in doing good, all possible good, in every possible kind and degree.

John Wesley

God often reveals His direction for our lives through the way He made us . . . with a certain personality and unique skills.

Bill Hybels

You are a unique blend of talents, skills, and gifts, which makes you an indispensable member of the body of Christ.

Charles Stanley

In the great orchestra we call life, you have an instrument and a song, and you owe it to God to play them both sublimely.

Max Lucado

A TIP FOR EMBRACING CHANGE

God has given you a unique array of talents and opportunities. The rest is up to you.

A MOMENT TO REFLECT

My thoughts about the importance of discovering—and using—my talents.

_____

_____

_____

_____

_____

_____

_____

_____

_____

_____

_____

_____

_____

Chapter 25

THE POWER
OF HOPE

I wait for the Lord;
I wait, and put my hope
in His word.

—

Psalm 130:5 HCSB

There are few sadder sights on earth than the sight of a man or woman who has lost all hope. In difficult times, hope can be elusive, but those who place their faith in God's promises need never lose it. After all, God is good; His love endures; He has promised His children the gift of eternal life. And, God keeps His promises.

Despite God's promises, despite Christ's love, and despite our countless blessings, we frail human beings can still lose hope from time to time. When we do, we need the encouragement of trusted friends, the life-changing power of prayer, and the healing truth of God's Holy Word.

If you find yourself falling into the spiritual traps of worry and discouragement, seek the healing touch of Jesus and the encouraging words of fellow Christians. If you find a friend in need, remind him or her of the peace that is found through a personal relationship with Christ. It was Christ who promised, "These things I have spoken unto you, that in me ye might have peace. In the world ye shall have tribulation: but be of good cheer; I have overcome the world" (John 16:33 KJV). This world can be a place of trials and tribulations, but as believers, we are secure. God has promised us peace, joy, and eternal life. And, of course, God keeps His promises today, tomorrow, and forever.

Let us hold on to the confession of our hope without wavering, for He who promised is faithful.

Hebrews 10:23 HCSB

Hope deferred makes the heart sick.

Proverbs 13:12 NKJV

Sustain me as You promised, and I will live; do not let me be ashamed of my hope.

Psalm 119:116 HCSB

For I know the thoughts that I think toward you, says the Lord, thoughts of peace and not of evil, to give you a future and a hope. Then you will call upon Me and go and pray to Me, and I will listen to you.

Jeremiah 29:11-12 NKJV

BE JOYFUL

Have you made the choice to rejoice? Hopefully so. After all, if you're a believer, you have plenty of reasons to be joyful. Yet sometimes, you may lose sight of your blessings as you wrestle with the challenges of everyday life.

Psalm 100 reminds us that, as believers, we have every reason to celebrate: "Shout for joy to the LORD, all the earth. Worship the LORD with gladness" (vv. 1-2 NIV). Yet sometimes, amid the inevitable hustle and bustle of life here on earth, we can forfeit—albeit temporarily—the joy that God intends for our lives.

If you find yourself feeling discouraged or worse, it's time to slow down and have a quiet conversation with your Creator. If your heart is heavy, open the door of your soul to the Father and to His only begotten Son. Christ offers you His peace and His joy. Accept it and share it freely, just as Christ has freely shared His joy with you.

I wish I could make it all new again; I can't. But God can. "He restores my soul," wrote the shepherd. God doesn't reform; he restores. He doesn't camouflage the old; he restores the new. The Master Builder will pull out the original plan and restore it. He will restore the vigor, he will restore the energy. He will restore the hope. He will restore the soul.

Max Lucado

Faith looks back and draws courage; hope looks ahead and keeps desire alive.

John Eldredge

I discovered that sorrow was not to be feared but rather endured with hope and expectancy that God would use it to visit and bless my life.

Jill Briscoe

Hope is nothing more than the expectation of those things which faith has believed to be truly promised by God.

John Calvin

Oh, remember this: There is never a time when we may not hope in God. Whatever our necessities, however great our difficulties, and though to all appearance help is impossible, yet our business is to hope in God, and it will be found that it is not in vain.

George Mueller

Love is the seed of all hope. It is the enticement to trust, to risk, to try, and to go on.

Gloria Gaither

People are genuinely motivated by hope and a part of that hope is the assurance of future glory with God for those who are His people.

Warren Wiersbe

A TIP FOR EMBRACING CHANGE

God has a plan for your life, a divine calling that you can either answer or ignore. How you choose to respond to God's calling will determine the direction you take and the contributions you make.

A MOMENT TO REFLECT

My thoughts about the power of hope and the rewards of trusting God.

_____

_____

_____

_____

_____

_____

_____

_____

_____

_____

_____

_____

_____

_____

Chapter 26

YOUR VERY BRIGHT FUTURE

*For I know the thoughts that
I think toward you, says the
Lord, thoughts of peace and not
of evil, to give you a future and
a hope. Then you will call upon
Me and go and pray to Me,
and I will listen to you.*

—

Jeremiah 29:11-12 NKJV

Because we are saved by a risen Christ, we can have hope for the future, no matter how troublesome our present circumstances may seem. After all, God has promised that we are His throughout eternity. And, He has told us that we must place our hopes in Him.

Of course, we will face disappointments and failures while we are here on earth, but these are only temporary defeats. This world can be a place of trials and tribulations, but when we place our trust in the Giver of all things good, we are secure. God has promised us peace, joy, and eternal life. And God keeps His promises today, tomorrow, and forever.

Are you willing to place your future in the hands of a loving and all-knowing God? Do you trust in the ultimate goodness of His plan for your life? Will you face today's challenges with optimism and hope? You should. After all, God created you for a very important purpose: His purpose. And you still have important work to do: His work.

Today, as you live in the present and look to the future, remember that God has a plan for you. Act—and believe—accordingly.

In all your ways acknowledge Him, and He shall direct your paths.

Proverbs 3:6 NKJV

For now we see indistinctly, as in a mirror, but then face to face. Now I know in part, but then I will know fully, as I am fully known.

1 Corinthians 13:12 HCSB

However, each one must live his life in the situation the Lord assigned when God called him.

1 Corinthians 7:17 HCSB

The earth and everything in it, the world and its inhabitants, belong to the Lord.

Psalm 24:1 HCSB

My cup runs over. Surely goodness and mercy shall follow me all the days of my life; and I will dwell in the house of the Lord forever.

Psalm 23:5-6 NKJV

LET GOD BE YOUR GUIDE

The Bible promises that God will guide you if you let Him. Your job, of course, is to let Him. But sometimes, you will be tempted to do otherwise. Sometimes, you'll be tempted to go along with the crowd; other times, you'll be tempted to do things your way, not God's way. When you feel those temptations, you must resist them, or else.

What will you allow to guide you through the coming day: your own desires (or, for that matter, the desires of your peers)? Or will you allow God to lead the way? The answer should be obvious. You should let God be your guide. When you entrust your life to Him completely and without reservation, God will give you the strength to meet any challenge, the courage to face any trial, and the wisdom to live in His righteousness. So trust Him today and seek His guidance. When you do, your character will most certainly take care of itself, and your next step will most assuredly be the right one.

The future lies all before us. Shall it only be a slight advance upon what we usually do? Ought it not to be a bound, a leap forward to altitudes of endeavor and success undreamed of before?

Annie Armstrong

Every experience God gives us, every person he brings into our lives, is the perfect preparation for the future that only he can see.

Corrie ten Boom

Our future may look fearfully intimidating, yet we can look up to the Engineer of the Universe, confident that nothing escapes His attention or slips out of the control of those strong hands.

Elisabeth Elliot

Fix your eyes upon the Lord! Do it once. Do it daily. Do it constantly. Look at the Lord and keep looking at Him.

Charles Swindoll

The Christian believes in a fabulous future.

Billy Graham

God's plan for our guidance is for us to grow gradually in wisdom before we get to the crossroads.

Bill Hybels

Are you serious about wanting God's guidance to become a personal reality in your life? The first step is to tell God that you know you can't manage your own life; that you need his help.

Catherine Marshall

A TIP FOR EMBRACING CHANGE

God will guide you if you let Him. You job is to acknowledge Him and to follow closely in the footsteps of His Son.

A MOMENT TO REFLECT

My thoughts about the bright future—and the eternal life—that is mine through Christ.

_____

_____

_____

_____

_____

_____

_____

_____

_____

_____

_____

_____

_____

Chapter 27

THE VALUE SYSTEM YOU CAN DEPEND ON

*Do what is right and good
in the Lord's sight, so that you
may prosper and so that you may
enter and possess the good land
the Lord your God swore to
[give] your fathers.*

—

Deuteronomy 6:18 HCSB

Whether you realize it or not, your character is shaped by your values. From the time your alarm clock wakes you in the morning until the moment you lay your head on the pillow at night, your actions are guided by the values that you hold most dear. If you're a thoughtful believer, then those values are shaped by the Word of God.

Society seeks to impose its set of values upon you; however, these values are often contrary to God's Word (and thus contrary to your own best interests). The world makes promises that it simply cannot fulfill. It promises happiness, contentment, prosper-

> Obedience is the outward expression of your love of God.
>
> —
>
> Henry Blackaby

ity, and abundance. But genuine abundance is not a byproduct of possessions or status; it is a byproduct of your thoughts, your actions, and your relationship with God. The world's promises are incomplete and deceptive; God's promises are unfailing. Your challenge, then, is to build your value system upon the firm foundation of God's promises . . . nothing else will suffice.

As a citizen of the 21st century, you live in a fast-changing world that is filled with countless opportunities to make big-time mistakes. The world seems to cry, "Worship me with your time, your money, your energy, and your thoughts!" But God commands otherwise: He commands you to worship Him and Him alone; everything else must be secondary.

Do you want to strengthen your character? If so, then you must build your life upon a value system that puts God first. So, when you're faced with a difficult choice or a powerful temptation, seek God's counsel and trust the counsel that He gives. Invite God into your heart and live according to His commandments. Study His Word and talk to Him often. When you do, you will share in the abundance and peace that only God can give.

You will know the truth, and the truth will set you free.

John 8:32 HCSB

God's Way is not a matter of mere talk; it's an empowered life.

1 Corinthians 4:20 MSG

Walk in a manner worthy of the God who calls you into His own kingdom and glory.

1 Thessalonians 2:12 NASB

Therefore, since we have this ministry, as we have received mercy, we do not give up. Instead, we have renounced shameful secret things, not walking in deceit or distorting God's message, but in God's sight we commend ourselves to every person's conscience by an open display of the truth.

2 Corinthians 4:1-2 HCSB

We must not become tired of doing good. We will receive our harvest of eternal life at the right time if we do not give up.

Galatians 6:9 NCV

IN DIFFICULT TIMES,
GOD TEACHES AND LEADS

Complete spiritual maturity is never achieved in a day, or in a year, or even in a lifetime. The journey toward spiritual maturity is an ongoing process that continues, day by day, throughout every stage of life. Every stage of life has its opportunities and its challenges, and if we're wise, we continue to seek God's guidance as each new chapter of life unfolds.

From time to time, all of us encounter circumstances that test our faith. When we encounter life's inevitable tragedies, trials, uncertainties, and disappointments, we may be tempted to blame God or to rebel against Him. But the Bible reminds us that the trials of life should be viewed as opportunities for growth: "Consider it a great joy, my brothers, whenever you experience various trials, knowing that the testing of your faith produces endurance. But endurance must do its complete work, so that you may be mature and complete, lacking nothing" (James 1:2-4 HCSB)

Have you recently encountered one of life's inevitable tests? If so, remember that God still has lessons that He intends to teach you. So ask yourself this: What lesson is God trying to teach me today?

God's love for His children in unconditional, no strings attached. But, God's blessings on our lives do come with a condition—obedience. If we are to receive the fullness of God's blessings, we must obey Him and keep His commandments.

Jim Gallery

Discrepancies between values and practices create chaos in a person's life.

John Maxwell

Trials and sufferings teach us to obey the Lord by faith, and we soon learn that obedience pays off in joyful ways.

Bill Bright

You will get untold flak for prioritizing God's revealed and present will for your life over man's . . . but, boy, is it worth it.

Beth Moore

If you want to be proactive in the way you live your life, if you want to influence your life's direction, if you want your life to exhibit the qualities you find desirable, and if you want to live with integrity, then you need to know what your values are, decide to embrace them, and practice them every day.

John Maxwell

We cannot rely on God's promises without obeying his commandments.

John Calvin

A TIP FOR EMBRACING CHANGE

When you place your faith in God, life becomes a grand adventure energized by the power of God.

A MOMENT TO REFLECT

My thoughts about the rewards of obeying God.

_____

_____

_____

_____

_____

_____

_____

_____

_____

_____

_____

_____

_____

Chapter 28

THE ULTIMATE PROTECTION

The Lord is my rock,
my fortress, and my deliverer.

—

Psalm 18:2 HCSB

The hand of God encircles us and comforts us in times of adversity. In times of hardship, He restores our strength; in times of sorrow, He dries our tears. When we are troubled, or weak, or embittered, God is as near as our next breath.

God has promised to protect us, and He intends to fulfill His promise. In a world filled with dangers and temptations, God is the ultimate armor. In a world filled with misleading messages, God's Word is the ultimate truth. In a world filled with more frustrations than we can count, God's Son offers the ultimate peace.

> There is not only fear, but terrible danger, for the life unguarded by God.
>
> —
>
> Oswald Chambers

Will you accept God's peace and wear God's armor against the dangers of our world? Hopefully so, because when you do, you can live courageously, knowing that you possess the ultimate protection: God's unfailing love for you.

The Lord bless you and protect you; the Lord make His face shine on you, and be gracious to you.

Numbers 6:24-25 HCSB

The Lord your God in your midst, the Mighty One, will save; He will rejoice over you with gladness, He will quiet you with His love, He will rejoice over you with singing.

Zephaniah 3:17 NKJV

God is my shield, saving those whose hearts are true and right.

Psalm 7:10 NLT

Those who trust the Lord are like Mount Zion, which sits unmoved forever. As the mountains surround Jerusalem, the Lord surrounds his people now and forever.

Psalm 125:1-2 NCV

Finally, my brethren, be strong in the Lord and in the power of His might. Put on the whole armor of God, that you may be able to stand against the wiles of the devil.

Ephesians 6:10-11 NKJV

YOU ARE PROTECTED

Although God has probably guided you through many struggles and more than a few difficult days, you may still find your faith stretched to the limit whenever you encounter adversity, uncertainty, or unwelcome changes. But the good news is this: even though your circumstances may change, God's love for you does not.

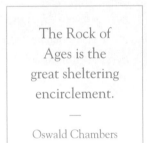

The next time you find yourself facing a fear-provoking situation, remember that no challenge is too big for your Heavenly Father. And while you're thinking about the scope of God's power and His love, ask yourself which is stronger: your faith or your fear. The answer should be obvious.

The Rock of Ages is the great sheltering encirclement.

—

Oswald Chambers

Wherever you are, God is there, too. And, because He cares for you today and always, you are protected.

A mighty fortress is our God, a bulwark never failing / Our helper He, amid the flood of mortal ills prevailing / For still our ancient foe doth seek to work us woe / His craft and power are great, armed with cruel hate, / Our earth is not his equal.

Martin Luther

Being loved by Him whose opinion matters most gives us the security to risk loving, too—even loving ourselves.

Gloria Gaither

The promises of God's Word sustain us in our suffering, and we know Jesus sympathizes and empathizes with us in our darkest hour.

Bill Bright

A TIP FOR EMBRACING CHANGE

When you invite the love of God into your heart, everything changes . . . including you.

A MOMENT TO REFLECT

My thoughts about God's love and His promise of protection.

_____

_____

_____

_____

_____

_____

_____

_____

_____

_____

_____

_____

Chapter 29

HE DOES NOT CHANGE

For I am the Lord, I do not change. Will a man rob God? Yet you have robbed Me! But you say, in what way have we robbed You? In tithes and offerings. You are cursed with a curse, for you have robbed Me, even this whole nation. Bring all the tithes into the storehouse, that there may be food in My house.

—

Malachi 3:6, 8-10 NKJV

God is eternal and unchanging. Before He laid the foundations of our universe, He was a being of infinite power and love, and He will remain so throughout all eternity.

We humans are in a state of constant change. We are born, we grow, we mature, and we die. Along the way, we experience the inevitable joys and hardships of life. And we face the inevitable changes that are the result of our own mortality.

But God never changes.

Is God the Rock upon which you've constructed your own life? If so, then you have chosen wisely. Your faith will give you the inner strength you need to rise above the inevitable demands and struggles of life here on earth.

Do the demands of this day seem overwhelming? If so, you must rely not only upon your own resources, but more importantly upon the Rock that cannot be shaken. God will hold your hand and

> When all else is gone, God is still left. Nothing changes Him.
>
> —
>
> Hannah Whitall Smith

walk with you today and every day if you let Him. Even if your circumstances are difficult, trust the Father. His promises remain true; His love is eternal; and, because He is the One who can never be moved, you can stand firm in the knowledge that you are protected by Him now and forever.

As God's children,
we are the recipients of lavish love—
a love that motivates us
to keep trusting even when
we have no idea
what God is doing.

—

Beth Moore

For you need endurance, so that after you have done God's will, you may receive what was promised.

Hebrews 10:36 HCSB

Whatever God has promised gets stamped with the Yes of Jesus. In him, this is what we preach and pray, the great Amen, God's Yes and our Yes together, gloriously evident.

2 Corinthians 1:20 MSG

What time I am afraid, I will trust in thee.

Psalm 56:3 KJV

God also bound himself with an oath, so that those who received the promise could be perfectly sure that he would never change his mind. So God has given us both his promise and his oath. These two things are unchangeable because it is impossible for God to lie. Therefore, we who have fled to him for refuge can take new courage, for we can hold on to his promise with confidence.

Hebrews 6:17-18 NLT

In a world kept chaotic by change, you will eventually discover, as I have, that this is one of the most precious qualities of the God we are looking for: He doesn't change.

Bill Hybels

Only believe, don't fear. Our Master, Jesus, always watches over us, and no matter what the persecution, Jesus will surely overcome it.

Lottie Moon

Our future may look fearfully intimidating, yet we can look up to the Engineer of the Universe, confident that nothing escapes His attention or slips out of the control of those strong hands.

Elisabeth Elliot

Worries carry responsibilities that belong to God, not to you. Worry does not enable us to escape evil; it makes us unfit to cope with it when it comes.

Corrie ten Boom

The promises of Scripture are not mere pious hopes or sanctified guesses. They are more than sentimental words to be printed on decorated cards for Sunday School children. They are eternal verities. They are true. There is no perhaps about them.

Peter Marshall

There is no safer place to live than the center of His will.

Calvin Miller

A TIP FOR EMBRACING CHANGE

Are you being tested? Call upon God. The next time you find your courage tested to the limit, remember that God is as near as your next breath, and remember that He offers strength and comfort to His children. He is your shield, your protector, and your deliverer. Call upon Him in your hour of need and then be comforted. Whatever your challenge, whatever your trouble, God can give you the strength to persevere, and that's exactly what you should ask Him to do.

A MOMENT TO REFLECT

My thoughts about God's unchanging promises.

_____

_____

_____

_____

_____

_____

_____

_____

_____

_____

_____

_____

_____

Chapter 30

SHARING YOUR TESTIMONY

God doesn't want us to be shy
with his gifts, but bold and
loving and sensible. So don't be
embarrassed to speak up for our
Master or for me, his prisoner.
Take your share of suffering for
the Message along with the rest of
us. We can only keep on going,
after all, by the power of God,

—

2 Timothy 1:7-8 MSG

Are you a believer who has made the decision to allow Christ to reign over your heart during these difficult days? If so, you have an important story to tell: yours.

In his second letter to Timothy, Paul shares a message to believers of every generation when he writes, "God has not given us a spirit of timidity" (1:7 NASB). Paul's meaning is crystal clear: when sharing our testimonies, we, as Christians, must be courageous, forthright, and unashamed.

Among the greatest gifts that we can give to our friends or family members is a willingness to share personal aspects of our faith. But sometimes, because we are fearful that we might be rebuffed, we may be slow to acknowledge the changes that Christ has made in our lives. Nonetheless, we must rise above our fears in order to share the story of Jesus with a world that desperately needs the healing touch of the Master's hand.

When we let other people know the details of our faith, we assume an important responsibility: the responsibility of making certain that our actions give credence to our words. When we share our testimonies, we must also be willing to serve as shining examples of righteousness—undeniable examples of the changes that Jesus makes in the lives of those who accept Him as their Savior.

Are you willing to follow in the footsteps of Jesus? If so, you must also be willing to talk about Him. And make no mistake: the time to express your belief in Him is now. You know how He has touched your own heart; help Him do the same for others.

———

There is nothing anybody else
can do that can stop God
from using us.
We can turn everything
into a testimony.

—

Corrie ten Boom

But sanctify the Lord God in your hearts, and always be ready to give a defense to everyone who asks you a reason for the hope that is in you.

1 Peter 3:15 HCSB

Whatever I tell you in the dark, speak in the light; and what you hear in the ear, preach on the housetops.

Matthew 10:27 NKJV

And I say to you, anyone who acknowledges Me before men, the Son of Man will also acknowledge him before the angels of God; but whoever denies Me before men will be denied before the angels of God.

Luke 12:8-9 HCSB

But as for me, I will never boast about anything except the cross of our Lord Jesus Christ, through whom the world has been crucified to me, and I to the world.

Galatians 6:14 HCSB

COMMISSIONED TO WITNESS

After His resurrection, Jesus addressed His disciples. As recorded in the 28th chapter of Matthew, Christ instructed His followers to share His message with the world. This "Great Commission" applies to Christians of every generation, including our own.

As believers, we are called to share the Good News of Jesus with our families, with our neighbors, and with the world. Christ commanded His disciples to become fishers of men. We must do likewise, and we must do so today. Tomorrow may indeed be too late.

You are the light of the world. A city that is set on a hill cannot be hidden. Nor do they light a lamp and put it under a basket, but on a lampstand, and it gives light to all who are in the house. Let your light so shine before men, that they may see your good works and glorify your Father in heaven.

—

Matthew 5:14-16 NKJV

Our commission is quite specific. We are told to be His witness to all nations. For us, as His disciples, to refuse any part of this commission frustrates the love of Jesus Christ, the Son of God.

Catherine Marshall

Witnessing is not something that we do for the Lord; it is something that He does through us if we are filled with the Holy Spirit.

Warren Wiersbe

To stand in an uncaring world and say, "See, here is the Christ" is a daring act of courage.

Calvin Miller

In their heart of hearts, I think all true followers of Christ long to become contagious Christians. Though unsure about how to do so or the risks involved, deep down they sense that there isn't anything as rewarding as opening a person up to God's love and truth.

Bill Hybels